LISIA MARIE'S BOOK

The Canary Handbook

Matthew M. Vriends, Ph.D.
Tanya M. Heming-Vriends

With Full-color Photographs
Drawings by Michele Earle-Bridges

BARRON'S

Dedication

For Kimy and Korrina
"Soyons fidèles à nos faiblesses."

All inquiries should be addressed to:
Barron's Educational Series, Inc.
250 Wireless Boulevard
Hauppauge, New York 11788
http://www.barronseduc.com

International Standard Book No. 0-7641-1760-2

Library of Congress Catalog Card No. 00-052956

Library of Congress Cataloging-in-Publication Data
Vriends, Matthew M., 1937-
    The canary handbook / Matthew M. Vriends, Tanya M. Heming-Vriends.
      p. cm.
    Includes bibliographical references (p.).
    ISBN 0-7641-1760-2 (alk. paper)
    1. Canaries. I. Heming-Vriends, Tanya M. II. Title.
SF463.V749   2001
636.6'8625—dc21
                               00-052956
                                 CIP

Printed in China

9 8 7 6

About the Authors

Matthew M. Vriends, a Dutch-born biologist/ornithologist, holds a collection of advanced degrees, including a Ph.D. in zoology. Dr. Vriends has written more than 100 books in three languages on birds and other animals; his detailed works on parrotlike birds and finches are well known. Dr. Vriends has traveled extensively in South America, the United States, Africa, Australia, and Europe to observe and study birds in their natural environment, and is widely regarded as an expert in tropical ornithology and aviculture. Dr. Vriends is the author or advisory editor of many of Barron's pet books.

Tanya M. Heming-Vriends was born in The Hague (the Netherlands) but came to the United States when still very young. She is a graduate of the University of Cincinnati, Ohio, and has worked with her father on various books.

Photo Credits

B. Everett Webb: pages vii, viii, 2, 3, 4, 5, 6, 7, 16, 27, 42, 45, 47, 52, 66, 76, 140, 144, 157, 163; J. G. Blasman: pages 10, 13, 20, 24, 29, 32, 55, 56, 57, 60, 61, 62 (left), 62 (right), 63, 64, 68 (left), 68 (right), 69, 70, 73, 74, 120, 121, 125, 126, 127, 128, 131, 132, 133, 134, 135, 136, 137, 138, 148, 150, 152, 153, 154, 156, 159, 164.

Cover Credits

J. G. Blasman: front cover, back cover, inside front cover, inside back cover.

Canary Varieties on Covers

Front Cover: left: Frosted Yellow (Gold); right top: Frosted Red-Orange; right bottom: European Canary; middle top: Non-frosted Yellow Female with Chicks; middle bottom: Yorkshire.

Inside Front Cover: Red-Orange Canaries.

Inside Back Cover: Recessive Silver Agate Opal Canary.

Back Cover: left: Yorkshire; top right: Hybrid European Canary x Green Canary.

Important Note

The subject of this book is how to take care of pet canaries. In dealing with these birds, always remember that newly purchased birds—even when they appear perfectly healthy—may well be carriers of salmonellae. This is why it is highly advisable to have sample droppings analyzed and to observe strict hygienic rules. Other infectious diseases that can endanger humans, such as ornithosis and tuberculosis, are rare in canaries. Still, if you see a doctor because you or a member of your household has symptoms of a cold or of the flu, mention that you keep birds. No one who is allergic to feathers or feather dust should keep birds. If you have any doubts, consult your physician before you buy a bird.

Contents

Preface

As canary breeders for many years, we have experienced the day-to-day problems that arise in a collection of birds; the same problems indeed that you, the canary fancier and reader of this book, also will experience.

This book functions as a general aid and guide for the canary fancier. It deals with the keeping, caring for, and diseases of canaries in great detail. Chapter by chapter, it hopes to enhance and increase the simple pleasures that the canary fancier experiences with his or her birds. The text provides the necessary information to breed canaries with greater success. It relates, explains, and gives examples. The more advanced fancier will also find information here, in simple language, that will enable him or her to breed more beautiful canaries.

There are no formulas in this book! Although logical and clear to those who can understand them and worthy in practice as far as breeding goes, formulas are much too complicated. Happily, it is entirely possible to learn about breeding color canaries and to understand simple genetics, without the use of complicated formulas. The secrets of heredity—which to the beginner are full of mystery and pitfalls—need not be the exclusive property of the experts.

We would like to acknowledge those who have helped in the preparation of this work. In particular we thank John Coborn for his ever unselfish assistance and support, without which this book never would have materialized. We would also like to thank the many canary fanciers at home and abroad who, over the years, have helped keep us in the forefront of "our" hobby. These include two well-known fanciers: Robert D. Dahlhausen, D.V.M., M.Sc. from Cincinnati, Ohio, undeniably one of our most eminent avian veterinarians, and J. G. Blasman from Rozenburg, the Netherlands, an excellent photographer and a most outstanding aviculturist; both have given their time to carefully study the manuscript and to make constructive remarks, for which we are extremely grateful. Any shortcomings in the text are our sole responsibility; we will gratefully receive any constructive criticisms or new ideas pertaining to this work.

New York, Matthew M. Vriends
Cincinnati, Tanya M. Heming-Vriends
Summer 2001

How Do You Become a Canary Fancier?

One of the greatest canary breeders we know, a man who in his life has bred many thousands of birds, often tells the story of how he became a canary fancier. He caught a vagrant canary hen that flew into his kitchen, and from this unlikely beginning, he became a stalwart of the fancy. His experience is not unlike that of our own; our "addiction" to the hobby also was triggered by a single hen. Once we did a survey, purely for interest's sake, to ask how various canary fanciers became involved with their hobby. Some answered that they had become fanciers just because they were attracted to canaries, and it was remarkable to hear how many fanciers had been influenced by this factor. Some had more or less inherited the hobby from their parents; others had friends or relations in the hobby and thus had become attracted to it, and still others had ended up with canaries via fancy chickens, pigeons, wild birds, or parakeets.

One person had found an aviary in his garden when he moved into a new house and had installed a pair of canaries, because he was, as he said, too lazy to pull the aviary down! Naturally there also will be a reason why you will want to become a canary fancier: the simple pleasure derived from an interesting hobby in

A beautiful lipochrome male.

your free time, the joy of hearing the clear tones of a singing canary, the delight in seeing your first nest of helpless youngsters, the satisfaction of a successful breeding season, the pride in winning an exhibition prize, and so on.

Genuine canary fanciers never have time to waste. They must care for their birds, they putter around building cages and aviaries, nest boxes, breeding cages, and flights. They enjoy their birds every day, they read about new aspects of the hobby, they talk about their birds with other fanciers. In short, they always have something to do and there is no question of boredom.

There are many things that can make your hobby even more interesting, but nobody can become a canary breeder overnight. You must go slowly but ever deeply into the noble art, and the deeper you go, the more it will fascinate you.

A good tip: Never stagnate in your hobby. Try to be always improving your knowledge and expertise of canaries and their breeding; this in itself will give you ever-increasing gratification. This book will help you derive pleasure from the hobby.

Victory March of the Canary

Many years have passed since Jean de Bethancourt (see page 75) placed the first canaries in a cage. These are years in which the canary has performed a victory march to all parts of the world. Never in history has a bird become so popular as the canary, and no songbird has ever been so intensively bred.

Why the canary was chosen as the most popular pet songbird is a mystery. Before the red factor canary was "discovered," there were many birds more colorful than canaries, birds that, with similar care and dedication as that given to the canary, could just as easily have been domesticated. Why, then, has just the canary become a domesticated pet?

One can, of course, look at a summary of the canary's attributes. It is not particularly shy and is extremely adaptable; it has a pretty song and attractive appearance; it breeds more readily than most other captive birds. It will thrive in almost any climate, and its requirements are simple.

But that is not all: The canary has attributes that are difficult to put into words, but that make it, more than any other bird, an ideal house pet.

Jean de Bethancourt's legacy then is millions of canaries bred over the years, making it the most prolific of all domesticated songbirds. The number of canaries in the United States alone is estimated to be four million!

The canaries bred over the years have brought as much joy to humans as the four million American birds are still bringing to us today. The various possibilities of canary breeding over the years have brought all fanciers what they want, whether it is for the song, color and the song, color and type, color and special feathering, large canaries, small canaries, multicolored canaries, and so on. And the repertoire is not yet complete; fanciers can still project new possibilities, new colors.

A red-factor male canary.

4

Love and dedication!

Whatever the canary is asked to do, it is willing to oblige. It is the friend of the quantity breeder as much as that of the specialist breeder. It raises its youngsters in sometimes adverse conditions. It demands nothing more than a little care, and rewards the fancier a thousand times for it. That is the secret of the canary, the secret of its popularity, and the secret that makes it breeding bird number one.

Love and Dedication

Without love and dedication to your hobby, it will come to nothing. If you turn to canaries just for something to do, then it is better if you don't begin rather than get bored later. Also, do not think that you will get rich from breeding canaries.

If you like birds in general, however, and you are drawn to canaries in particular, if you have love, dedication, and ongoing enthusiasm to take the canary fancy seriously—to regard it as a hobby and sacred pastime, rather than a means of making a profit—then you have the makings of a good fancier.

Canary keeping is going to cost money, how much depends on what you want to spend. If you want to start big—build and buy lots of cages and aviaries, purchase the best of everything—then the hobby will cost you a lot of money, especially at the beginning. But if you decide to make a small and sensible

There are type canaries, and...

entry into the fancy, it will not need to cost a great deal at all. You can quite easily make a serviceable breeding cage and purchase one or two breeding pairs of canaries.

Then if you barter or sell any youngsters you breed and use the money to buy better canary stock, your improvements are still not going to cost you much and a modest purse will allow you to build a reasonable aviary. As long as you don't overdo it with the numbers of canaries you obtain, your feeding budget will be remarkably low, even with the extra food requirements at breeding time.

Possible Profit

Once you have mastered the task of becoming a full-fledged canary breeder, which will take up much of your spare time and spare room, it is not out of the question that you will earn a small profit. And, over the years, theoretically, at least, it even may be possible to make a reasonable sum of money with your canaries.

That is, theoretically; in practice, you often get a totally different result. Take, for example, the retired pensioner who, at age 65, felt too young and fit to spend the rest of his life at leisure. He already had many years of experience as a canary breeder, so he decided to set up a large-scale canary breeding project. This retired man did not take any undue risks. He had carefully worked out a budget. The prices of cages, the cost of losses, the cost of feeding, and the average prices he hoped to receive for his birds were all reckoned. Even the costs of extra heating and lighting in the winter were not left out.

He estimated to make about $1,800 to $2,500 in an average year,

...color canaries.

and in a bumper season to make perhaps $3,000 or more. He carried on his project for four years before he had to close up shop. In the first year he had broken even; in the second year he made a profit of $875, the third year a loss of $200, and the fourth year he broke even again. So for four years of hard work, he had made a net profit of just $675!

He was not particularly disappointed, however; in those four years he had not just simply earned $675, he had kept himself fully occupied with his hobby. The pleasure alone this gave him must have been worth a lot of money.

No, the canary fancy is not a profit spinner. Without dedication, there is no point in starting. Those who look at their birds with dollar signs in their eyes are on the wrong track. Of course this does not mean that you must not be realistic. As you breed successfully, you expand and get some reward for your dedication. And when you have surplus canaries, it is natural that you will want to get the best possible price for them. If you are successful, then you sometimes can expect a reasonable return at the end of the year. Regard such a profit as a bonus and don't imagine it will be a sure thing every time.

Of course, all breeders have the right to carry out their hobby in the way they best see fit. Some see having a large number of birds as the key to breeding success. Others specialize in particular birds—for color, for song, or for conformation. They believe in the pure hobby, without thought of profit. These are the happiest fanciers, as they see the hobby as it really is—a pleasurable pastime.

There are many other kinds of fanciers: the man who has a single canary in a cage near the window, the city man who has built a tiny aviary in his small backyard, the woman who has a breeding cage in her living room where she can enjoy the wonder of egg laying, brooding, hatching, and rearing. These are all real fanciers. They all enjoy their birds in their own way—feeding and caring, probably enjoying their hobby more than the man with 100 birds.

Acquiring Canaries

The acquisition of birds is the beginning, and the way you begin can mean the difference between success and failure. Start with a good ground rule: Only the best is good enough for the beginner!

Of course, the person who wants a single pet canary to keep in a cage in the living room probably will have a different set of standards than the person setting out to breed perfect offspring; the former can be satisfied with the song and the color of his canary without it having to be a champion. But of course, his bird also must be healthy.

Consider a man who is going to breed from his birds. For him, the quality of the prospective acquisitions is of the greatest importance, bearing in mind that his first birds are the beginning of a new stud line. These will decide whether his breeding efforts will be a success or failure

and, in many cases, these birds will be the answer to whether a fancier remains one or not.

Is it necessary for a beginner, therefore, to start with a pair of very expensive, perfect red-orange canaries? No, the novice needs to start with something simpler, with "ordinary" green, yellow, or variegated canaries. They are not expensive and they have no special demands. It really doesn't make any difference whether your canary is of a particular color, has frilly feathers, or is an exceptionally enthusiastic singer. Buy the bird that appeals to you the most.

Of course, not every bird lover will turn out to be a canary breeder. If you discover after a couple of years that canary breeding is not for you, then nobody will be hurt. Your short "affair" with the hobby will have not cost much money.

The First Canaries

The first "general canaries" purchased must be regarded by the fancier as study material. You can gain experience in caring for these birds in and out of the breeding season, how to deal with brooding and rearing, what demands the birds have with housing and so on. And after a couple of seasons, when you have mastered the keeping and breeding of canaries, the way to the canary fancy "high school" is now open.

You therefore should buy the best quality bird that you can afford. Don't go for inferior quality just to save, say $25. If possible, always go to a trustworthy canary breeder or dealer. If you do not know either, it is recommended that you attend one of the bird shows that are organized by societies once or twice a year in most major cities. At such a show you can see the quality of birds, you can meet breeders and dealers, and you can gain all sorts of useful knowledge and advice, including the addresses of supply sources.

It is even more appropriate to become a member of a canary or cage bird society, because then you will be in regular contact with other fanciers—both beginners like yourself and those who have had many years of experience.

Never hesitate to ask for advice when you can get it. If you haven't much personal experience with canaries, you won't know what is good and what isn't. However, if you take an experienced fancier with you, he or she will be able to advise you on what is worth purchasing. By just looking at the bird, a fancier will be able to tell you if it is fit and healthy; by holding the bird he or she will be able to tell you what sex it is and whether it is suffering from any disease.

If you want to try on your own, however, consider the following advice: Buy only from breeders or dealers who have their cages and aviaries in top condition. It is likely that the birds will be sound and healthy.

Breeders

The breeder who is conscientious in one aspect is likely to be in all others, but if you see that the premises are dirty and untidy, you should decline politely, turn your back, and walk out again.

A good breeder already will have banded the surplus birds and will, of course, have kept some kind of a studbook. He or she usually will be able to tell you some of the birds' immediate histories and whether any of their ancestors were champions. *It is best to obtain birds that were hatched in the spring or summer*, as these are nearly always superior to birds born in fall or winter. Such information will be available from the studbook.

The Healthy Bird

You must know what a healthy canary looks like.

1. A healthy bird sits upright on its perch and behaves in a sprightly and nimble manner.

2. Its eyes are bright and gleaming, it has sleek, tight plumage, and it does not allow other birds in the cage to bully it.

3. Take such a bird in the hand and examine it from the tip of its beak to the tip of its tail. The beak must close properly and should be smooth in texture. Examine the top of the head, which should show no bald patches. Check the wing feathers for damage, and make sure that the tail is not soiled. Look at the feet one by one; they should be smooth and clean. The toes must be straight and complete with claws; old birds will show signs of calcium deposit.

A non-frosted yellow hen on her nest with her partner, also non-frosted yellow, keeping guard.

4. The breastbone runs down through the center of the breast. Feel the flesh on either side of the breastbone and press gently but firmly with thumb and forefinger. It should feel plump and firm, not hollow, wiry, or flabby, with the breastbone's keel prominent, like a blade.

5. Examine the vent and surrounding area. If this is dirty and matted with droppings and stains, the bird may be suffering from some kind of enteric disease, so, for obvious reasons, it should be discarded as a choice. For similar reasons, other birds in the same or adjacent cages should not even be considered.

6. Hold the bird's breast against your ear and listen to its breathing. If it is healthy, you probably won't hear much at all; if it has a respiratory infection, however, you will hear a rasping and squeaking noise and the bird should be refused.

7. Blow the feathers on the breast open; the skin you see should be clean and healthy-looking, not spotty or red, or dry and flaky, which can be a sign of external parasites.

If the canary passes all the above criteria with flying colors, then you can be almost sure that the bird is healthy.

Of course, not all bad symptoms are necessarily fatal to canaries. There are treatments for these and other diseases, but you do not want to worry about unpleasant diseases at this early stage. Always buy the best and healthiest you can afford.

Male or Female?

How do we distinguish the sexes of canaries? There are no obvious external sexual characteristics, at least not to the eyes of a novice, to whom a yellow canary is a yellow canary and a green one is a green one. Those who have been "in the trade" a bit longer, however, will begin to recognize the subtle differences between the cock and the hen by carefully appraising the birds. For a start, the cock frequently is brighter in color than the hen, which applies to all colors except white. Of course, this will help only if there is comparison material, and even the experienced expert will find it difficult to sex a single bird by just looking at its plumage.

Fortunately, there are other characteristics, but the bird first must be taken in the hand, holding it belly up and blowing the feathers around the vent to one side. If the vent is smooth and round, it is a hen (in the breeding season, the vent is oriented to the rear and has a torpedolike form). In the cock, there is a small, pimplelike swelling next to the vent, the *seminal vesicle*, which serves for temporary storage of semen.

Beginners may find some of this difficult because they will not know precisely where to look and how to interpret what they see. It is therefore best to enlist the help of a more experienced fancier—someone in your bird club will be willing to help—to teach the finer art of sexing.

It can be more difficult to sex younger birds, because the characteristics are not so obvious. Even experts have identified a young bird as a hen that later suddenly turned out to be a cock. When sexing young canaries, it is therefore best to wait as long as possible and try to get it right the first time.

One characteristic should not be forgotten: the song. Even this is not infallible, however, as some young cocks and hens will sing very similarly. However, there is no mistaking the full adult song of the canary cock.

When to Buy Canaries

In theory, canaries can be acquired at any time of the year, but in practice, there are certain points that first must be taken into consideration.

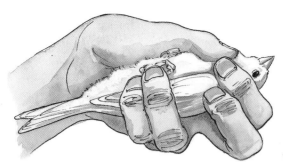

If you have to examine your bird, place your thumb on one side of the canary's head and your other fingers on the opposite side of its head and body.

For a start, any bird that has been kept inside or in a heated aviary throughout the winter cannot be placed outside as soon as you purchase it. It would soon succumb to a bad cold or even worse. Fanciers with outside aviaries, therefore, should buy birds from outside aviaries only during the colder parts of the year. There are no reverse problems; a bird from outside can be placed in a warm, indoor situation with no worries as long as light and ventilation are adequate.

The best times to acquire new birds are during late spring, summer, or early fall when there is no great difference between indoor and outdoor temperatures, at least not enough to cause health problems. There are other problems in late spring and summer, however; at these times canaries are usually in short supply as most birds are in the throes of breeding. The only birds available are likely to be weaklings or birds that in some way are unsuitable for breeding. It is thus best to buy the current season's youngsters in the early fall. Do not wait until too late in the fall before acquiring birds as these will be too young to breed in the next season. Moreover, the earlier fall birds will give you the greatest choice from the earlier clutches of the season. Those in later broods are often of inferior quality.

This advice relates to birds from breeders, most of whom sell their birds to pet stores. There are some breeders who may wait until the spring before selling and are then able to hike the price—but of course, it costs money to keep birds through the winter, and there is a risk that some may die, so most breeders dispose of their surplus stock before winter sets in.

How to Manage Canaries

There must be many potential fanciers who have not yet asked themselves the question "How do we manage our birds?" Real bird lovers, however, may have a natural gift for dealing with birds; they will learn easily, and new things will come naturally to them.

When dealing with birds, be calm and quiet; in their presence, you must do everything you can to avoid frightening them: no shouting, no sudden movements, and no unusual situations. Keep the following in mind:

When dealing with canaries, be calm and quiet, especially in a bird room with breeding pairs.

1. The calm fancier who respects his or her birds will have calm birds. He or she will speak softly to the birds when near them or entering the aviary. Speaking to the birds is important; they will grow accustomed to the calm voice and will know that the "boss" is coming and there is no need for alarm as the fancier likely will be bringing them food and water.

2. When the boss puts his or her hand in the breeding cage to replenish the rearing food, the birds will remain calm, as the hand will not alarm them; a soft, calm voice will reassure them that there is nothing to fear.

3. This is, of course, especially important with breeding birds. During the breeding season (and out of it for that matter), the conscientious fancier also will beware of even the apparently simplest of indiscretions. For example, if he or she enters the breeding aviary every day without a hat, he or she should not suddenly go in wearing one—this could cause more stress and trouble than one could imagine! Canaries are really quite sensitive birds, as they—compared to dogs and cats, for example—have not been domesticated for long.

4. Canaries will indeed breed in small spaces in the house, but these will be birds that already are accustomed to small spaces. A breeder who allows everyone into the breeding room naturally can permit himself or herself more indiscretions than the person who receives only a few visitors through the breeding season. But it is recommended that, while the birds are brooding and rearing, as few strangers as possible be allowed in the breeding room or aviary. There are birds that will object to visiting strangers, with possibly disastrous consequences.

Netting Birds

Occasionally it will be necessary to remove a bird from its cage or aviary. This can be a difficult process that needs to be carried out with great care. If you are too rough, the bird will be stressed and possibly injured; if you are too careful, it can take too long and the birds will be stressed anyway. As a general rule, canaries should be handled as little as possible. They really hate it and it can stress them a lot. If the bird is in a small cage, it is best caught in the hand. First, reach your hand into the cage, hold it still for a few moments until the bird settles, then quickly place your hand gently but firmly over the whole bird.

In larger cages or aviaries, it is best to use a net with a diameter of about 10 inches (25 cm) and a depth of 14 to 16 inches (35–40 cm), which can be purchased from avicultural suppliers, but is quite easy to make your own with a piece of curtain material and a padded wire. The handle should be about 20 inches (50 cm) long, perhaps more if you have a particularly high aviary.

It usually is easiest to catch the birds in flight when using such a net and, this way, there is less chance of injuring them. Netting birds should be done with a minimum of fuss and as quickly as possible. If you allow it to develop into an extended "hunt," you will do a lot of damage.

If you have to catch several birds from an aviary, do it in two or three trips. It is better to spend two lots of five minutes than one lot of ten minutes. A short catching time is less stressful for the birds.

Many breeders have found dead birds in their aviaries after an extended effort at trying to catch birds. This, of course, is an example of how easy it is to stress birds and how serious stress is.

Chapter Two

Accommodations for Canaries

Canaries have been domesticated for quite some time; they will adjust to almost every situation—feeling at home in a small cage in the house, in an indoor flight, or in an outdoor aviary with shelter. They will reproduce in a breeding cage or in an aviary, and it does not make a lot of difference where the breeding cage is situated. Canaries have been bred in family rooms and kitchens, in conservatories and lofts, and even in a basement, although the latter is not actually recommended as being an ideal place to breed canaries.

A single canary in a cage in the house can give you years of pleasure. There have been reports of canaries reaching 15 years of age in a fancy or "household" cage—and that is the bird's entire life!

The canary has no great demands. As long as its food dish is regularly filled, and its water is fresh, and as long as it gets an occasional tidbit of green food, such as chickweed, and some cuttlebone, then it is happy.

It is quite remarkable what owners give their pet canaries to eat. Frequently they eat "out of the pot" and they are given bits of meat, potato, chips, cake, cookies, sugar, and all sorts of things. This is not good. There are some fanciers who will swear by a piece of bacon fat, but there is no benefit from this; it just makes the bird thirsty.

Of course, you can feed your canaries what you wish, but if you want to keep your bird fit and healthy it must have a balanced diet and adequate exercise.

The Cage

The canary has no great demands when it comes to cages. Of course, a large cage, preferably a long one, is better than a small or high cage, as the bird will have more freedom of movement in the former. Such a cage placed near a window, where it will get a bit of sun, will keep the canary healthy and happy, and encourage it to sing. If you recently have acquired a canary, place the cage at eye height for a few weeks; this will help the bird feel more comfortable. After

A frosted male at ease in his "home."

a few weeks you can then move the cage higher or lower if you wish. Always beware of drafts; do not place the cage in a drafty area. If the window near the cage needs to be open, move the cage so it is not in the full blast of a draft.

Sometimes cages are placed high above the window, but this is the wrong place as the ranges of temperature are too varied high in the room. In the winter, when the heat is on, the heat rises to the ceiling and when those in the room are nice and warm, the canary can be nearly cooking! When the heat is lowered at night, or when the door is left open for ventilation, the canary can be suddenly and dramatically cooled; such sudden changes can cause stress and all sorts of complications, such as bowel disturbances or an unseasonal molt. A sort of continuous molt or "soft molt," with the unfortunate result that the feath-

ers never achieve perfect development, is often the result. The birds keep on losing a few feathers, soon cease to sing, and gradually get into a poor state of health. Exposing canaries to too much artificial light may also cause soft molt; to avoid this, the cage should be partially covered with a dark cloth. Canaries also do not like cages that move in the draft.

Of course, in good weather, there is no reason why the canary cage cannot be placed outside. A canary that spends most of its time inside surely will benefit from a little fresh air and sunshine.

Unsuitable models: A large variety of cages can be seen in pet stores, most built with the proposed tenants in mind. However, there are some models that are totally unsuitable for canaries, for example, the popular "tower" upright cage, which is probably only suitable for a couple of lovebirds or small tropical finches. Fancy cages with vertical bars are well suited to canaries, whereas those with horizontal bars are best left to hook-beaked parakeets and parrots. Although as much room as possible is preferable for the birds, this does not mean you should not consider the smaller cages. Breeding successes are not guaranteed, but fanciers who want a single pet bird are not interested in breeding anyway; their main priority is to obtain a good singing bird. They are not likely to be participating in exhibitions or canary singing competitions. They really just want the bird to provide some companionship and interest in their home and perhaps to serve as a topic of conversation when visitors arrive.

Cage Varieties

The many varieties of cages offered in the avicultural trade change, and usually improve, from one year to the next. Fortunately, the days of a canary fancier placing a bird in a tiny cage with hardly enough room for it to turn around are over. Currently available cages are usually large, attractive, often finished in chrome and glass, and have colorful and hygienic plastic bases that avoid rust (where bacteria and other undesirables could lodge) and help stop seed and other debris from being strewn all over the carpet. As the base is easily separated from the upper part of the cage by undoing a few little hooks, there is no need to catch the bird at cleaning time. The top is simply removed with the bird on its perch and placed on a sheet of newspaper while you clean the base in no time at all. In fact, the base can be easily washed with lukewarm water and detergent, rinsed, and wiped dry in a matter of a minute or so. The main body of the cage will be provided with access doors so that you can easily remove perches for cleaning and sanding at regular intervals. The seed, water, and bath containers usually are serviced from outside the cage as they are affixed over special openings in the wire, thus causing a minimum of disturbance to the bird. You can purchase special stands from which the cage can be

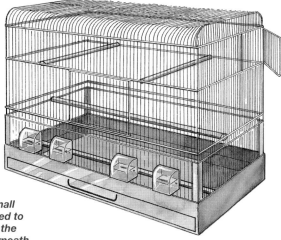

A large, long cage is better than a small or high one. Perches should be spaced to prevent the droppings of the bird on the top perch from soiling the bird underneath.

Cages

The length of the cage is of prime importance. It is best to stick to the following *minimum* sizes:

- *Fancy* (household) *canary cage*: 19½ × 14 × 16 inches (50 × 35 × 40 cm); wires must be set 19 gauge—½ × ½ inch (12.5 × 12.5 mm), no more.
- *Cage for type canary*: 23½ × 19½ × 23½ inches (60 × 50 × 60 cm).
- *Canary breeding cages*:
    1. *Single breeder*: 14 × 12 × 16 inches (50 × 30 × 40 cm).
    2. *Double breeder*: 28 × 12 × 16 inches (100 × 30 × 40 cm). This cage is divided into two parts by means of a wooden or wire slide.
    3. *Triple breeder*: 42 × 12 × 16 inches (150 × 30 × 40 cm) by means of two such slides. By thus dividing the cage into three parts, a male canary can be kept in the center part, and by removing either of the slides, it can be run with either hen. After the breeding season, both slides can be removed and one has an excellent flight cage for the hens.

suspended, but these are not recommended, as the cage will swing at the slightest draft, shock, or movement—not designed to give a bird peace of mind! A cage should be placed preferably at eye level or higher; a bird feels happier if it is looking down on you, in a manner of speaking.

At the present time, there are so called "French" cages on the market, usually white, antique-looking, with pitched roofs, wrought iron decorations, and so on. Though it is often difficult to see the bird in such a cage, there is no objection to it as long as there is adequate room inside.

With regard to cage sizes, type canaries (canaries whose standards are based on their conformation and the posture with which they stand) require more room and thus larger cages than those required by song and color varieties.

Fancy Clothespins

The fancy pegs or clips made of colored plastic or wood, and about 4 inches (10 cm) long used for holding memos can be very useful to the canary fancier. They can hold a cage door open and secure greens or pieces of fruit or vegetables. They can even be used as additional perches, bearing in mind they can be moved at any time to any part of the cage. They can have similar uses in the aviary and no doubt there are many more possibilities that you may discover.

Perches

Perches should be fashioned preferably from good hardwood, such as oak or beech. They should be oval, and about ⅜ to ¾ inch (1–2 cm) in diameter. The bird's foot should encircle it comfortably. Perches that are too thin provide no abrasion and thus allow the bird's nails to grow too long; this will cause the bird a lot of discomfort, and you the inconvenience of having to clip them at frequent intervals. Perches also should not be too smooth in texture; a rough, natural surface will help keep the nails worn to a respectable length. By rubbing the perches with coarse sandpaper about once a week, you will ensure roughness. "Sandy" and "Biomagnetic" perches, available in most pet stores, are good for keeping claws worn to a suitable length and eliminating painful foot pressure points. A perch always should be placed within easy reach of the food and water containers. A couple of perches near the top of the cage will be used at bedtime as canaries, like most birds, like to roost at the highest point available. However, make sure that they are not so high that the bird's head touches the cage ceiling; otherwise it may end up with a bald patch!

Do not place too many perches in the cage as the birds must have adequate room to move about and exercise. Also, do not place perches one above the other as a bird sitting above can soil the perch—or another bird—below. For similar reasons, do not put the perch directly over a food or water container, or too near to the cage wire. It is a good idea to have perches of varying thicknesses (about ⅜ to ¾ inch [1–2 cm], for example) so that the muscles of the birds' feet and legs get plenty of exercise.

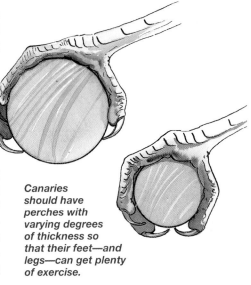

Canaries should have perches with varying degrees of thickness so that their feet—and legs—can get plenty of exercise.

Location

Cages or aviaries in which one or more canaries are kept will need adequate light during the day and as much sunshine as possible, but allow the bird to be able to get into shade at all times if it wishes. Thus, rooms and gardens with a northerly aspect are not ideal places for cages or aviaries. A mistake often made by the beginner or prospective fancier is to imagine that some little dark alcove in the house will be an "ideal place to put a cage." Don't even consider it unless it gets plenty of direct window light and at least an hour of sunshine each day. Even if daylight and sunshine are substituted with fluorescent lights and sunlamps, the birds will still suffer the consequences sooner or later. We do not mean to suggest that the birds would not survive for a few years in such situations; they certainly could, but that is not the point. In our opinion, and it should be that of everybody who keeps birds, the main objective should be in keeping

Type canary show.

the birds' condition at its highest peak. Birds that don't get a full quota of sunlight soon will lose the luster in their plumage, the brightness of their colors; they will be slowly pining away their lives. All too frequently, lovely and expensive birds housed in such a manner slowly die, in spite of having all their other requirements provided.

The care of birds can be compared with that of houseplants. No matter how much is known about the plants and no matter how careful you are in making sure they get all their other requirements, without adequate light, and with some species direct sunlight, you soon can expect that they will die.

It is thus a major requirement that at least part of the *front of a cage* (a box cage in which only the front has bars) or aviary *faces south.* If this is not possible, then face the cage as near to south as you are able, and preferably southeast rather than southwest. If the front does not face wholly south, it is a good idea to have part of the aviary front covered with glass or transparent plastic. The aviary also should be placed in a sheltered spot, preferably surrounded with subtle plantings of flowers and shrubs to enhance the interest and attraction of it.

Indoor cages and aviaries also should, preferably, look out at a large, south-facing window (the larger the better) and again, if south is not possible, then southeast is preferable to southwest so that the birds can enjoy a few hours of sunshine every day. The suitable indoor situations are also ideal spots for indoor plants. Use your artistic talents to arrange the plants and birds into an interesting and attractive focal point.

Box Cages

All birds like a certain amount of privacy and therefore will be much happier in a cage that is mainly closed. The box cage is just as its name suggests—a box with a wire mesh or bar front, giving the bird maximum privacy and reducing the prospects of "threats" arriving from most directions. However, it is very important that such a cage is placed in a light situation. You must be careful when doing this, as a box cage soon can become a heat trap if left in the full sun. Make sure, therefore, that it always has at least partial shade. Another safety precaution is to drill a few neat holes in the roof of the box at the rear, to allow any stagnating hot air to escape.

Because they offer so much privacy, box cages are *ideal for breeding pairs*. Many people place their box cages in entrance halls and corridors. There is nothing wrong with this, providing you keep them out of excessive drafts, which will occur particularly where doors are continually being opened and closed. Canaries can be stressed by cold drafts, which can be the start of all sorts of problems.

The Cage Base

All well-designed cages should have a removable tray with a grate at the base, which can be taken out for cleaning. Most of the more decorative types of cages obtainable in pet stores have removable plastic bottoms or sliding metal trays. Box cages should have a shallow tray covering the whole floor that slides out through a narrow gap at the base of the bars. The floor tray is best covered first with some heavy paper (brown wrapping paper is ideal), then a 1-inch (2.5-cm) layer of clean sand or mini corncob, both available in various brands in your pet store. Every week the floor coverings should be replaced. To prevent sand, seed, and husks from being kicked excessively out of the cage, a piece of glass about 4 inches (10 cm) high can be affixed around the bottom edge of the cage. Of course, with designer cages, these are already provided.

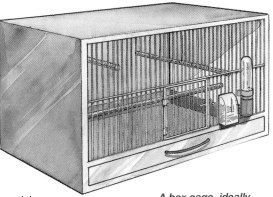

A box cage, ideally suited for breeding canaries because it offers much privacy, should be placed in a light, draft-free location.

Some of the More Common Potentially Poisonous Houseplants

Amaryllis	(*Amaryllis* species)	Hydrangea	(*Hydrangea macro phylla*)
Autumn Crocus	(*Colchicum* species)	Japanese Yew	(*Taxus cuspidata*)
Azalea	(*Azalea* species)	Java Beans	(*Phaseolus lunatus* var.)
Balsam Pear	(*Memordica charantia*)	Lantana	(*Lantana species*)
Bird of Paradise	(*Poinciana gilliensii*)	Lilly-of-the-Valley	(*Convallaria majalis*)
Boxwood	(*Buxus* species)	Narcissus	(*Narcissus species*)
Caladium	(*Caladium* species)		
Castor Bean	(*Ricinus communis*)	Nightshade (Deadly, Black, Garden or Woody Nightshade, and Eggplant [all except fruit])	(*Solanaceae*)
Chalice Vine	(*Solandra species*)		
Coral Plant	(*Jatropha multifida*)		
Daffodil	(*Narcissus* species)		
Datura (berries only)	(*Datura* species)	Oleander	(*Nerium species*)
Dieffenbacia	(*Dieffenbachia picta*)	Philodendron	(*Philodendron species*)
Elephant's Ear	(*Colocasia* species)	Rhododendron	(*Rhododendron species*)
Hyacinth	(*Galtonia* species)	Yam Bean	(*Pachyrhisus erosus*)

Covering the Cage

Although many fanciers believe it is kind to cover the cage of their pet canary with a cloth at night, the canary itself is not always of the same opinion. The best method is to just partially cover the cage so that no direct light shines on the bird. That way the bird can choose whether or not it wants to sit in the light.

Possible Dangers

It is recommended that caged pet canaries be regularly allowed free flight in the room. However, take great care that there are no potential pitfalls that could be a danger to your pet.

1. Windows and doors must be kept closed for obvious reasons. The windows should be covered with draperies to prevent the bird from flying into the glass—possibly having fatal results.

2. Mirrors should be covered or removed for the same reason.

3. Electrical appliances including heaters, stoves, and so on must be turned off.

4. Ceiling fans are especially dangerous, so be sure they are off when the bird is out.

5. Make sure the open fire is out or guarded and that there is no escape route up the chimney.

6. Houseplants and cut flowers can be a danger to your bird. If there is any chance that a plant may be poisonous, remove it from the room before the bird comes out. Cacti can be responsible for wounds; the bird could get its feet caught in the spines, for example. These should be removed or covered with plastic before the bird is allowed out.

7. Other pets, like dogs and especially cats, cannot be trusted with your birds. Sometimes the pet will appear to be the best of pals with your feathered friends when you are present, but turn your backs and birdie soon can become just another item on the doggy menu!

8. Do not place cages on windowsills or high up on a cupboard too close to the ceiling. It is preferable to affix a special shelf for the cage, just above head height.

9. If several cocks are kept in different cages in the same room, the cages should be placed so that the birds cannot see each other. The songs of cock birds will decline quickly if they can see other cocks. Separate hens also should not be in view of the cocks for similar reasons.

10. Never place a canary cage too close to or in front of a TV set; the continual flickering of the TV picture is bad for the bird's little eyes. The farther away from the TV set the better, preferably even in a separate room. Research has shown that it is best to cover the cage when the TV is on, and that the distance between the TV and cage should be not less than 16 feet (5 cm).

Cleaning the Cage

A cage must be kept spotlessly clean. A buildup of dirt also may mean a buildup of pathogenic

TV

A canary—or any other bird for that matter—never should be exposed to television. A German scientist investigated the theory of harmful rays and found that there were none! He found, however, that birds see television as a series of blinding flashes or, in other words, detect the rapid changes of dot patterns on the screen. So if you have a television in the same room as your canary, be sure to shield the cage when the distance between the cage and the TV set is less than 16 feet (5 m).

Breeding box cage with a pair of apricot canaries (the male is intensive, the hen is half intensive).

week. Food and drinking and bath-water containers should be cleaned with hot water and soap at least once a day. It is best to make cleaning a routine job, carried out, for example, every Saturday morning. All items, as already indicated, should be washed in hot soapy water, rinsed, and dried before being reassembled. Broken and cracked feed containers should be discarded and replaced as they can harbor bacteria and other unpleasant organisms. You probably will have to remove the bird for this procedure, so why not do the cleanup when it is having its recreational flight around the room? With several birds and cages, you will have to have a spare cage in which to put the canaries while cleaning is in progress. By placing doors together, you usually can coax the birds easily from one cage to the next without the need to handle them. Breeding birds should not be removed from their cages or unduly disturbed; make do with just cleaning the floor tray and utensils during this period.

organisms dangerous to the health of the birds (and sometimes even to humans!). The cage, perches, food and water containers, bath, food clips, and so on all should be given a thorough once-over about once a

Frilled canaries should be sprayed with a mister.

Bathing Facilities

Many wild birds, including wild canaries, like to bathe by rolling around in wet grass. If there is a grassy area in your outdoor aviary, you may be able to experience the pleasant sight of your canaries gamboling in the morning dew. Birds in cages and indoor aviaries do not have this pleasure, but they still

Washing your canary: Immerse the bird carefully in a shallow bowl of warm soapy water, about 77°F (25°C). Apply soap, if necessary.

enjoy a bath. Miniature plastic or metal "bathhouses," made to be affixed against the open cage door, can be purchased in pet stores. Your canaries usually will make good use of the shallow water provided, splashing and flapping, getting the cool water right down to the skin, which must give them a good feeling, as they will come back for more time and time again. However, once a day is usually adequate and, after the canary's first bath, it is best to remove the water. Otherwise, the sand on the floor of the cage may become a soggy mess.

Before a Show

If you are going to enter your birds in a show, it will be necessary for you to give them a good bath about a week beforehand.

1. Prepare two shallow bowls of warm water about 77°F (25°C), dissolving a little mild soap in one of them. A good brand of dishwashing detergent is ideal.

2. Take the bird in your hand, so that the thumb and forefinger are gently but firmly restraining its little head.

3. Lower the bird into the soapy solution, but keep the head dry and make sure that no fluid gets into the eyes, beak, or nostrils.

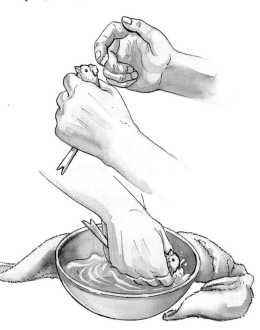

Wash the head with your finger or a shaving brush. Make sure that no fluid enters the eyes, beak, and nostrils. "Rinse" in clean, warm water.

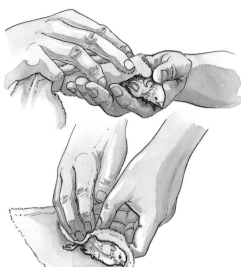

Dry off all excess water with a warm towel. Or "roll" the bird in a warm cloth or towel.

7. Dry the bird, possibly using a soft, warmed towel, stroking it in the direction of the tail. Then place in a cage (without sand, or if the cage has a grate, only paper should cover the bottom) in a warm, draft-free indoor place, never outside in the sun. Leave it there for 24 hours to allow the bird to thoroughly dry out. Some fanciers use a hair dryer, but this must be done with great care, as too much heat will cause the feathers to curl, as well as result in stress to the bird, which can be accidentally burned.

Summer Care

Whatever kind of birds you keep, hygiene is of utmost importance. Cleanliness is especially important during the warmer times of the year. Soft foods (universal food, rearing food, water-soaked bread, greens) will spoil much faster than you may think. Parasites and other nuisance insects will breed much faster, promoting the rapid growth of bacteria. And, however strange it may sound, do not ignore the possibility of canaries suffering from heatstroke! Daily inspection of all birds and their accommodations is therefore essential.

Birds that spend most of the year indoors will benefit from an occasional excursion outside their cages during the spring and summer. Do not place the cage in full sun, however. Also, do not place the cage where it will be in danger of interference from dogs, cats, and other bird enemies. If you keep cats, you will

4. Dunk it in the water a few times until its feathers are thoroughly wet. Then wet an old soft-haired shaving brush or similar item in soapy water, and brush the plumage in the direction of the tail. The head and neck can be wiped gently with a soft sponge. Once again, take care not to get any soap in the eyes, nose, and beak.

5. The wing feathers can be spread out over the edge of the bowl and thoroughly brushed. Do the tail feathers in the same manner. Be very gentle however as you do not want to pull any feathers out—a detriment to show canaries!

6. Once the bird has been soaped thoroughly, it can be rinsed off in the clear water. You can dunk your canary a few times, then brush its plumage back into shape.

Open cage, roomy enough to start a family.

need to be on constant alert. As a special treat you can allow your canary to forage in the grass by placing the cage, minus the bottom, on the lawn. However, it is advisable to stay with the bird when you do this. Of course, this should be done only on lawns that have not been fertilized or otherwise chemically treated.

What Your Canaries Need from You

The preceding text may make you think that a canary in a cage requires very little in the way of care and feeding. Indeed, these colorful and charming little songsters certainly do

not make any great demands. By providing them with a daily quota of good-quality seed, fresh drinking and bathing water, weekly treats of chickweed, lettuce, or spinach, and a little calcium (a cuttlebone hung permanently in the cage will take care of that requirement), they will be grateful enough.

Warning: Although this care and feeding schedule is not necessarily perfect, it is far better than the so-called "care" some people give their pet canaries. It is not advisable to give the birds any starchy and fatty foods from your table. Strangely, the canary will accept gratefully what is offered, but this does not necessarily mean it is good for the bird; it will become overweight and lethargic, especially if it doesn't get much exercise. Therefore, as ornithologists and aviculturists, we would recommend, for the sake of your pet's health, that these "treats" gradually be eliminated.

Community Aviaries

Canaries are quite suitable as cohabitants of a community aviary. A community aviary is one in which a number of compatible (nonaggressive) bird species are kept together for ornamental purposes. Canaries are not at all inclined to be aggressive toward other small exotic birds, making them an excellent and colorful choice in your community. This does not of course mean that canaries are "wimps." A couple of male canaries in a cage together are likely to fight constantly if you are not careful. Strangely, however, three or more males together will live in harmony, as their basically innocent pursuits and threatening gestures will then no longer mean anything.

Conversely, you should make sure that other birds in the aviary do not terrorize the canaries. As a rule of thumb, only birds of a similar size or smaller than the canaries should be kept with them and you also should make sure that these are not bullies. Even some tiny bird species can be absolute thugs if given the chance. We once kept a brambling (*Fringilla montifringilla*) in an aviary together with canaries. It turned out to be a real little terrorist towards some of the male canaries and it

literally mopped the floor with them. It had to be removed immediately, carefully of course, but this shows how you must watch out for hostile attitudes and rectify them before it is too late. You must be particularly watchful whenever new specimens are introduced to the aviary.

In general, it is not considered advisable to keep canaries together with budgerigars or other parrotlike birds. These hook-beaked birds have a rather nasty habit of aiming for the feet in acts of aggression and their strong beaks can cause a lot of damage. Although parrots and parakeets can defend themselves against each other, canaries and other songbirds are at somewhat of a disadvantage, so keep the budgies separate.

If you are serious about breeding your canaries, do not expect them to be too successful in a community aviary. Canaries like peace and quiet when breeding, so it is best to keep the number of other birds to a minimum.

Like most birds, canaries prefer to choose their sleeping sites as high up as possible and they will squabble like mad to get the best roosts. Therefore, always make sure there are adequate high-up roosting perches for *all* of the birds, plus a few surplus ones just in case. The perches should be located fairly close (but not too close for soiling) to the wall and in a cozy, draft-free spot. It is unlikely that the nightly settling down proceedings will ever be completely peaceful, but this should eliminate most of the problems.

A charming little garden aviary.

To avoid quarrels over food, it is best to have two or three food/water stations in the aviary. Peace and tolerance in a community aviary is very important. Continual bickering soon can cause stress in some of the birds and breeding successes will be reduced to nil.

When using a community aviary for breeding purposes, there should be several choices of nesting boxes or nesting pans, preferably twice as many facilities as there are pairs of birds. To avoid arguments, keep the nesting facilities as far apart as possible.

The Outdoor Aviary

Aviaries can be erected indoors, perhaps in a separate room, in the loft, or even in the basement, but in most cases they are erected outdoors and include a night shelter. The size of the aviary will depend on the amount of space available and sometimes on the cost, but it is wise to make it as large as possible. A night shelter, which will serve as sleeping quarters and protection from inclement weather, is essential. It is important, therefore, that such a shelter be totally rainproof and well insulated against drafts. It also should be sufficiently large, in case the birds have to be kept inside for longer periods, as in snap cold spells, for example. It is also recommended that part of the outside flight be covered with solid (transparent plastic) panels so that the birds can shelter out of the rain without going

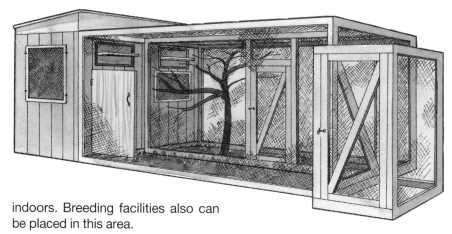

indoors. Breeding facilities also can be placed in this area.

Designs

There are many designs for aviary construction and every person has his or her own preferences. How you construct your aviary is, of course, up to you, but you only have to go and look in the backyards of many city dwellings to see how aviaries should *not* be constructed. In many cases, canaries are kept in shaky, dilapidated hovels, built from all kinds of odd bits of packing cases, corrugated iron, various-sized meshes, and so on, all botched up together to form constructions that certainly are not a credit to the builders. However, the surprising thing about all this is that many of the canaries bred in these monstrosities often turn out to be excellent show specimens.

By all means, use secondhand materials to construct your aviaries and night shelters, but in the interest of aesthetics, please try to make your aviary an attractive addition to the garden, rather than something

A double outdoor aviary with a safety porch (right). You may cover part of the mesh roof (or the whole roof) with corrugated plastic to keep out the droppings of wild birds, and to help protect your birds from cats and birds of prey.

that sticks out like a sore thumb. You do not have to be the perfect handyperson to construct an original, attractive, and serviceable aviary, but if you are absolutely hopeless with your hands, then seek out the help of somebody who isn't. The following notes should help give the do-it-yourselfer an ideal aviary, which you can, of course, adapt to your own specifications.

Location

Always pick a spot that faces as near to south as possible and, if not due south, southeast is preferable to southwest. The site should be as level as possible for ease of construction. Choose a spot in the garden that allows you to enjoy your aviary as much as possible, preferably one surrounded by flowers and shrubs and ideally where it can be seen easily from a window in the house. If the aviary backs onto the wall of a garage, shed, or other outbuilding, or even a wall of the house, all the better, as it will provide ready-made shelter. Before erecting any structure however, make sure that you are not violating any local laws; in some areas it may be necessary to obtain building permits from your local authorities. Also, consider members of your own household and neighbors. Have a discussion with your family and come to an agreement first; tell your neighbors what you intend to do and ask if they have any objections, such as noise or blocking a view. It is infinitely better to sort these things out at the beginning!

Materials

There is almost no limit to the number of types and sizes of aviaries

A roomy, simple garden aviary with a safety porch. Try to face the front south, preferably where flowers, bushes, and trees will frame the aviary.

suitable for canaries. Perfectly suitable small aviaries made completely from metal, or timber framed, can be purchased from avicultural suppliers or directly from the appropriate manufacturers. Many fanciers, however, prefer to build their own aviaries to their own patterns. The reason for this is that it is often difficult to fit a prefabricated aviary into a particular spot, whereas it is much simpler to build one to measurements. Some manufacturers supply single aviary panels that easily can be bolted together in all shapes and sizes, and these will save you a lot of time. The cheapest way, however, is to build your own aviary completely from scratch, providing you have the time and the expertise. Aviaries can be built from all kinds of materials, but if you are building your own, the timber-framed one is probably the easiest. Though such a framework can be placed directly on the ground, it is always worth going to the trouble of laying a solid foundation, such as concrete, paving stones, etc. There

are several good reasons for this, the least of which is that it will provide for a more professional and attractive finish. It will prevent predators and vermin from burrowing into the aviary and creating havoc among your birds, and it will mean that the wooden structure will not come into direct contact with the soil, thus reducing the possibility of wet or dry rot, termites, and so on from attacking the wood.

Construction

Although the size of the aviary is up to the individual fancier, imagine here, for convenience sake, that you are going to construct an aviary with a flight approximately 13 × 6½ feet (4 × 2 m) and a shelter 6½ × 6½ feet (2 × 2 m) which would easily accommodate about six pairs of canaries and perhaps a few exotics as well.

Foundation: Dig out a foundation trench to a depth and width of 14 inches (35 cm). For this example aviary it would be 19½ feet (6 m) along each side and 6½ feet (2 m)

along each end, allowing for the bases of the aviary framework to run along the center. A further 6½-foot (2-m) trench may be dug across the width at the proposed junction between the flight and the shelter. If you use wooden pegs, a straight edge, and a spirit level, you can find a constant level all around. Then you may pour concrete (a good mixture is one part cement, two parts sharp sand, and four parts gravel mixed with water to a workable consistency) into the trench up to the top of the leveling pegs, then tamped and troweled. When it is partially set, scratch a key in the surface to help hold the cement for the brickwork.

The wall: Allow at least 24 hours for the foundation concrete to set, before building a low 12-inch (30-cm) high wall with bricks or concrete blocks cemented together with mortar, all around the foundation and across the junction between the flight and shelter. In order to secure the aviary framework, a number of bolts should be cemented in between the bricks and pointing vertically upwards at intervals of about 12 inches (30 cm). Allow 48 hours for the mortar to set before proceeding.

The shelter floor: The shelter floor should be partially filled with rubble, then sand, and covered with a sheet of dampproofing plastic, then filled in with about 4 inches (10 cm) concrete to the top of the wall to make a solid floor. Some fanciers like the floor of the flight also to be of solid concrete, but personally we like to leave this natural for planting.

A roomy garden aviary for canaries.

Panels: Either purchased or do-it-yourself aviary panels consisting of good quality treated 2 × 2 inches (5 × 5 cm) or 2 × 3 inches (5 × 7.5 cm) timber should be used. Minimum height should be about 6½ feet (2 m), making your aviary this height plus the height of the wall. It is easier to fit the wire mesh (galvanized steel with ½ inch [1.5 cm] mesh is best) to the flight panels before they are erected. These are nutted onto the bolts you have on top of the foundation walls and then bolted together as you go along, the roof panels going on last. Part of the outside flight can have a transparent, corrugated plastic roof with a similar panel down the front, to make a sort of sheltered but still external area between the flight and night shelter.

The shelter is built from similar panels but without wire of course. These panels are covered with weatherboard or similar material on the outside, and lined with some kind of paneling—plywood, chipboard, nonasbestos insulation—on the inside, and it is a good idea to have insulation material in the cavity. The shelter should have large windows facing south and these should be lined on the inside with mesh.

Paint: The inside of the shelter should be painted with lead-free, washable paint. A light color will enhance the daylight effect, show off the birds better, and give an incentive to keep things clean.

Roof: The roof of the shelter should preferably be insulated with a ceiling inside, and may be covered simply with bituminous roofing felt, corrugated, galvanized steel sheeting, or, to make it more attractive, roofing tiles or shingles. The roof should slope away from the flight and away from fences, walls, and so on. If necessary, you can erect a gutter and drainpipe to lead rainwater away to a drain or perhaps to collect in a barrel.

Entrance: The entrance to the night shelter should have a safety porch, a tiny "entrance hall" with double doors. You enter and close the outside door before opening the interior mesh door to join the birds and thus make sure there are no escapes. Another plan is to make a small "inspection" corridor about 30 inches (75 cm) wide in the shelter, separated from the birds by mesh doors. The bird area can be divided in half horizontally so that the birds use the top half, making it easier for you to clean the floor regularly as it will be just above waist height. The area below also can be divided in half, vertically this time, one half for storing bins of food, spare feeders, and so on, the other half for putting in cages for isolated birds.

Door: The door to the flight can be at the other end of the "corridor" while the birds themselves move between the two areas through a pophole, which should be situated fairly high up in the wall between the flight and shelter. The hole need be no greater than 8 × 8 inches (20 × 29 cm), and a narrow shelf should be fitted at its base so that canaries can take off and land as they use it. A sliding door can be fitted over the pophole, so that the birds can be locked up in bad weather or kept in for easier catching, and so on. The door can be fitted into vertical grooves and pulled up from outside the aviary by means of a chain, passing it through a piece of metal pipe bent to shape. The door is held open by securing the chain on a hook; take care not to trap birds under the door when you release it. Some fanciers prefer to lock their birds in the shelter every night, and in the winter this is not a bad idea. In the summer, however, especially in the breeding season, canaries like to be out and about at dawn so it is then best to leave the pophole open.

Decorating the Aviary

Along with the essential furnishings—feed and water dishes, feeding platforms, perches—the aviary can be made more attractive by decorating it, inside and out, with plants. Trees and shrubs not only enhance the look of an aviary, they offer some shelter from inclement weather. Moreover, the birds like to spend a lot of time outside in the sunshine during the summer, but not necessarily in the direct rays of the sun. With ample shrubbery in the aviary, they can enjoy the outdoor life without becoming stressed from too much sunlight. A natural arrangement of shrubs and plants also gives the birds a sense of privacy and security, enabling them to breed with more determination. If your outdoor flight is concreted over (some

fanciers prefer this for the purposes of hygiene and the total exclusion of rodents), you still can have some shrubs inside. These are grown in large pots or tubs. One advantage is that if you have a spare set of plants in tubs, you can change them every couple of months, allowing those from the aviary to have a period of rest and recuperation in the garden before changing them again.

We personally prefer a natural floor in the outdoor flights. This can be turfed or seeded with grass. You must allow the grass to become established before you introduce the birds. A couple of areas can be planted with flowers and shrubs, preferably toward the back and ends of the flight, and always making sure that there is still plenty of free-flying space.

Following is a list of hardy shrubs that are easy to care for and ideal for planting in and around a garden aviary. Try to choose a mixture of evergreen and deciduous trees and shrubs so that you have some foliage all year-around.

Common juniper (*Juniperus communis*): An evergreen conifer that can grow to 32 feet (10 m) or more, but still will flourish if occasionally cut back. It can take on interesting shapes especially if trained by pruning and wiring. The needles are arranged in small wreaths in groups of three. It does well in poor soil and provides thick cover in the aviary. Several other Juniperus species also make ideal aviary plants.

European larch (*Larix decidua*): Unusual in being a deciduous conifer; however it is an attractive tree, with soft green, lacy foliage hanging on weeping branchlets. In fall, the needles turn a glowing gold and brown before dropping. It grows well in poor soil and responds to pruning.

Silver fir (*Abies alba*): A particularly attractive evergreen that will do well even in poor sandy soil. The needles are a shiny, dark green, with two, bluish white stripes running along the bottom side, giving the whole tree a silvery appearance when viewed from a distance. The closely related Nordmann fir (*A. nordmannia*) has longer needles attached in a brushlike arrangement. It is an ideal aviary shrub in its juvenile form.

Spruce fir (*Picea excelsa*): A hardy evergreen that has needles up to 1 inch (2.5 cm) long and is individually attached to the branches. They are dark green in color and the buds are resin-free. The trunk is straight, with branches starting right at the bottom. The Norway spruce, (*P. abies*) is another attractive species, useful in the aviary in its younger forms. There are also many attractive cultivars in the *Picea* genus.

Douglas fir (*Pseudotsuga taxifolia* or *P. menziesii*): This fir has needles forming two rows that are ⅔ to 1⅓ inches (18–33 mm) long. These are a lovely pale green on top, and gray-green beneath. There are tiny resin knobs that appear irregularly on the bark. This tree can grow as tall as

General Remarks on Aviary Construction and Maintenance

• When making the foundation, wire mesh can be placed additionally on either side of the concrete below ground to further help keep out mice and rats, and if you don't construct a solid foundation, this is essential.

• Some fanciers stretch mesh over the whole of the flight floor area beneath the turf about 6 inches (15 cm) below the surface.

• Metal wires also can be used to add strength to concrete foundations and walls.

• Be sure that solid roofs extend over the edges of the walls at all points.

• If you intend to build adjacent aviaries or flights for parrotlike birds, be sure to have a double mesh wall between them to prevent the hookbeaks from nipping at a canary's foot that may happen to be sticking through the wire.

• Wire mesh painted in mat dark green or black cuts out glare and enables you to watch your birds with more comfort.

• After painting, allow to dry completely before introducing any birds. Only use child-safe paints. Old-fashioned whitewashing is not considered safe, as it may flake and the birds could pick up chips with harmful chemicals.

300 feet (90 m) and to 13 feet (4 m) in diameter, so only young specimens are suitable for the aviary.

Scotch pine (*Pinus sylvestris*): A tree that prefers sandy, heathlike habitats. Small specimens make hardy and attractive trees in the aviary. The firm, evergreen, bluish green needles grow in small bunches and can reach 3 inches (8 cm) in length. The reddish brown bud seldom secretes resin. The Austrian or black pine (*P. nigra*) has even longer, up to 6 inches (15 cm), very dark green, paired needles, making it a very decorative tree. The bud produces resin. Young specimens are useful in the aviary.

American arborvitae (*Thuja occidentalis*): Excellent hedging material that can soon be trimmed into shape. It is ideal for making a wind break, especially in community aviaries with tropical birds. The leaves are dark green on top and lighter beneath, scallop-shaped, and appear in a cross design. In the past, young ladies used to place a small twig of this species inside a handkerchief in order to enjoy the pleasant scent that emanates when it is rubbed a little. This North American tree, if allowed, will grow up to 50 feet (15 m) in height. It is now grown in many parts of the world. The oriental arborvitae (*T. orientalis*) is similar but the leaves are the same green above and beneath. Originating in the Far East, it also is now grown in many parts of the world.

Common privet (*Ligustrum vulgare*): From southern Europe and Asia Minor, it is so adaptable that it has become a pest of endemic proportions in some countries where it has been introduced. Needless to say, it is very hardy and an ideal evergreen cover shrub in the aviary. It also makes an excellent hedging plant. The sturdy, lanceolate leaves are deep green; there is also a golden variegated variety. The wood is hard, and during spring it blooms with a profusion of tiny white flowers.

Common boxwood (*Buxus sempervirens*): An evergreen tree that originated in the Mediterranean region. The small oval leaves reach a maximum of 1 inch (2.5 cm) and have a leathery texture. They are dark green on top and have a silvery sheen beneath. It is an excellent hedging or shaping plant, much used in topiary in Old World gardens, which provides dense cover. It is rather slow growing but this can be advantageous in the aviary.

Japanese spirea (*Spiraea japonica*): An ideal aviary plant as it has numerous branches, forming dense cover. It is a deciduous shrub that grows to about 6 feet (2 m). The leaves are sharply toothed and lanceolate, growing to about 4 inches (10 cm) in length. It has flattened, 6-inch (15-cm) wide heads of small white or pink flowers, borne on erect stems in late summer.

False spirea (*Sorbaria sorbifolia*): A Siberian native and thus very hardy. Growing to 10 feet (3 m) in height, small specimens are ideal for the aviary. It has yellowish white

Aviary plants. Top: Common juniper (left) and Norwegian spruce (right). Bottom: Scotch pine (left) and Douglas fir (right).

flowers arranged in bunches in late summer.

Snowberry (*Symphiocarpus albus*): A deciduous shrub native to North America. It has knotty branches on which some exotic birds like to nest. The leaves are broadly ovate and pale to mid-green. It has small pink flowers in July through September, followed by white berries that some birds like to eat.

English ivy (*Hedera helix*): An evergreen creeping plant that is useful for growing up posts or covering walls. The younger leaves have three to five lobes; those on the mature branches become oval or diamond-shaped. The leaves are leathery in texture and come in a range of color varieties including light and dark green, white veined, and variegated. In late fall and winter it develops bluish black berries from the insignificant flowers. Ivy provides nesting sites for some tropical birds, which also enjoy eating the berries.

European elderberry (*Sambucus nigra*) and **common elderberry** (*S. canadensis*): Both are hardy shrubs that have bunches of strongly scented white flowers in June and July. The leaves are dark green and the black berries that follow the flowers are enjoyed by many birds. For some reason, elderberry seems to be a great attraction to aphids, those tiny sap-sucking insects that can be such a nuisance in the garden. In the aviary, however, these aphids will provide a valuable animal protein food supplement for the birds, which will eagerly seek them out among the foliage. Indeed, an occasional aphid-infested branch from elsewhere can be placed in the cage or aviary as a supplementary food source and this will be especially beneficial through the breeding period.

English hawthorn (*Crataegus monigyna*): A deciduous shrub native to Europe and a classical inhabitant of English hedgerows. The bright green leaves are deeply indented and the branches are dense and thorny, providing excellent cover and nesting sites. In fall, the red berries are enjoyed by many birds.

Rambling rose (*Rosa multiflora*): Barely needs description. It is well suited for growing both inside and outside an aviary, forming attractive, dense cover and providing good nesting sites.

Rhododendron (*Rhododendron ponticum*): A beautiful shrub that comes in many varieties. The leaves of most rhododendrons are poisonous, so these plants are unsuitable for parrotlike birds. However, as the leaves are leathery and rather tough, they are unlikely to be any hazard to canaries, finches, or softbills. Smaller specimens make dense, colorful shelters for birds in flights. As they prefer to grow in acid soil, a good amount of organic material such as peat, placed around the root ball at planting time, will do much to promote growth and flowering.

Oregon holly grape (*Mahonia aquifolium*): A commonly grown evergreen shrub from North America. Growing to a height of about 3 feet (1 m), it is ideal for the aviary. The glossy, dark green, leathery leaves are oval and hollylike, with prickly edges; they change to dark red as winter approaches. The fragrant, rich yellow flowers are borne in dense clusters in March to April, and are followed by tight bunches of bullet-shaped, blue-black berries that birds enjoy. This plant is very hardy and will do well in most soils and conditions.

European hornbeam (*Carpinus betulus*): Another deciduous tree that grows to 50 feet (15 m) but kept well pruned it makes an ideal dense hedge in which small birds like to nest. The short-stemmed, oval leaves are doubly indented and soft green, turning yellowish brown in fall, and persisting well into the winter, though spells of extra cold weather will cause them to drop suddenly.

There are many other choices of aviary plants; in fact the choice is almost endless. Useful species include: *Cotoneaster* (all varieties), *Viburnum* species, various *Vaccinium* species including the cranberry (*V. oxycoccus*), the highbush or swamp blueberry (*V. corymbosum*), the lowbush blueberry (*V. pennsylvanicum* or *V. augustifolium*), and the cowberry or foxberry (*V. vitis-idaea*). Then there is the sea buckthorn (*Hippophae rhamnoides*), the mock orange (*Philadelphus coronarius*), and the

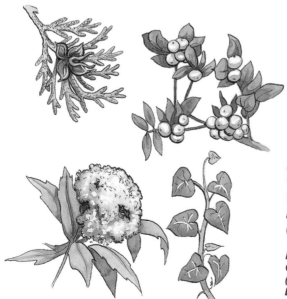

Plants for outdoor aviary. Top: Chinese or Oriental arborvitae (left) and Snowberry (right). Bottom: Japanese spirea (left) and English ivy (right).

Aviary plants (clockwise from top left): English hawthorn, common elderberry, rosebay rhododendron, and shrub rose.

various Genistra species, including African broom (*G. monosperma*), dwarf broom (*G. sagittalis*), creeping broom (*G. pilosa*), and dyer's greenweed (*G. tinctoria*).

Just as with plants in the garden, aviary plants will require regular care and maintenance. They will require watering well in long dry spells. A sprinkler will benefit both the plants and the birds, which will frolic in the wet foliage. Occasional cultivation and fertilization around the base of shrubs will be necessary, and great care should be taken to prune trees and shrubs *before* they start damaging the aviary wire. If tree trunks should get rather thick, it is a sign that the roots may start damaging the aviary foundation, so the whole tree should be taken out and replaced before that stage is reached.

The Room Aviary

This is a room inside the house that has been turned over to the birds. Like the outdoor aviary, it should have a little entrance porch, though there will be no need for a night shelter. The room should be well lit, with windows preferably facing south. Some supplementary lighting may be used in dark corners. Such a bird room often is used by breeders of color and song canaries and it is also very good for other species of tropical and subtropical birds. It is possible to keep a few of the rarer species together with the canaries, providing of course that they are compatible. Expensive species, such as Australian grass finches or the larger humming birds, really do well in such a room aviary.

Some fanciers like to divide their room aviary so that there is a large flight, plus an area for breeding cages, equipment, and so on. Quite often a room aviary can be more efficient and appropriate than an outdoor one, especially for those who have a spare room that they can devote to their hobby. Naturally, you will need to plan well in advance to help make the room aviary (or bird room) effective and enjoyable. The floor preferably should consist of paving stones or something similar.

The room can be enhanced with plants and shrubs in pots and tubs that are changed frequently for rest and recuperation. A little artistic license will create a bird room in which you can spend many pleasurable hours. Install a bench or seat where you can sit restfully and watch the antics of your birds.

The Indoor Aviary

Unlike the bird room or room aviary, in which the whole room is used for birds, an indoor aviary is actually a large, decorative indoor cage in a corner of a room. The indoor aviary is ideal for the fancier who is not over ambitious, or does not have a garden space for an aviary. It is ideal for those who just wish to keep and breed a small number of birds. You can buy ready-made indoor aviaries. We have seen many with casters that can be moved easily from one location to another. The best, however, are those that are purposely built into a position in the room that is as undisturbed as possible; with some forward artistic planning, such an aviary can be very attractive indeed. We have seen indoor aviaries that were beautifully set up and in which birds bred successfully, even though children played daily on the floor and at a table less than 3 feet (1 m) away from the nesting pans. Of course, your breeding successes are likely to be even better if the aviary is placed in a more peaceful situation, but this goes to show that everybody can have the pleasure of bird keeping, even with the minimum of facilities.

General Maintenance

In addition to the maintenance of aviary plants, there are a number of chores that must be carried out on a regular basis. Sand used on the floors of night shelters and indoor aviaries must be replaced regularly, about once a week, and especially

A large indoor aviary.

when it is unpleasantly soiled with droppings, seed husks, and so on. In the outdoor aviary, areas of open soil must be regularly turned, and areas of worn turf dug out and replaced. Twice a year, just before and just after the breeding season, perches, sleeping quarters, and all inside surfaces should be scrubbed, disinfected, and hosed down. If possible, it is best to house the birds in temporary cages while all this is going on, allowing you to really clean inside and out, repair leaks, drafty cracks, and faults in the wire, prune shrubs, and otherwise bring everything back into top form.

If you bring your birds inside for the winter, that is the time to give the outdoor aviary a thorough going-over so it will be ready for the next season. If this procedure is repeated faithfully each year, you will be unlikely to be surprised by a great many problems at any one time. Winter is the best time to thoroughly clean and repair nest boxes, pans, and so on. Feeding and water hoppers, baths, etc. should, of course, be cleaned very frequently. For this reason, such utensils should be placed in the cage or aviary where it is easy to service them without disturbing the birds too much. A small hatch in the aviary wire or in the wall of the shelter, with a little feeding/watering platform just behind it is ideal; you can then service food and water without entering the aviary. By keeping your aviary as clean as you can, both you and your birds will benefit.

Commonly Used Disinfectants

• *Lysol*: Manufactured by Lehn and Fials Products, Div. of Sterling Drug, Inc.
Dilution: 4 ounces per gallon (118 ml per 3.7 L) water.
All-purpose disinfectant.
Available through grocery stores, veterinarians, or janitorial supply houses.
• *One-Stroke Environ*: Manufactured by Vestal.
Dilution: ½ ounce per gallon (15 ml per 3.7 L) water.
All-purpose disinfectant; official disinfectant of the USDA.
Available through grocery stores, veterinarians, or janitorial supply houses.
• *Clorox*: Manufactured by the Clorox Co.
Dilution: 6 ounces per gallon (177 ml per 3.7 L) water.
May be irritating to skin; may be corrosive to bare metal. Excellent for concrete flooring.
Available through grocery stores, veterinarians, or janitorial supply houses.
• *Betadine*: Manufactured by Purdue-Frederick, Inc.
Dilution: ¾ ounce per gallon (8 ml per 3.7 L) water.
Excellent noncorrosive disinfectant, but more expensive.
Available through veterinarians.

Note: Always follow manufacturers' recommendations.

Chapter Three
Feeding Canaries

Basic Feeding Requirements

Canaries are natural seedeaters, as can be seen in their strong, short, and wide beaks that are designed to pick up and dehusk seeds. Their special digestive systems also are designed to deal with mainly vegetable foods. Canaries are able to obtain all of their essential dietary constituents—proteins, carbohydrates, and fats (macronutrients), also vitamins and minerals, including trace elements (micronutrients)—from a mixture of seeds and green food, plus a little animal food and grit. There is no single kind of seed in which all of these dietary essentials occur in sufficient amounts, so a seed mixture is necessary to make the diet of your birds as varied as possible.

Proteins

The most important group of macronutrients consists of proteins, which are used in the body for the growth, repair, and replacement of body tissues. Proteins also are nec-

Variegated Fife Fancy canaries.

essary to aid the performance of various bodily functions, and include enzymes, hormones, and antibodies. Proteins form the most important part of the egg; they must be present in the diet of the developing chick as well as the adult. Proteins are indeed so important that a deficiency of these nutrients in the diet will cause an immediate loss of condition and deterioration in health. It is estimated that about 12 percent of a canary's diet must consist of proteins, so the greatest portion of the food must be protein-rich seeds—namely, canary grass seed and rape.

All proteins are built up with various forms of amino acids, which are changed by various enzymes, such as pepsin, into other acceptable forms of amino acids during digestion. These amino acids can then be transported around the body in the bloodstream until they can be used somewhere in the tissues. There are about 24 different amino acids, but, fortunately, the canary does not require all of them. It gets by with about 10 and also can manufacture some in its own body.

As a seedeater, the canary misses out on the excellent animal proteins found in insects, and so on. Such proteins generally are easier to absorb than vegetable proteins. Canary breeders use this fact by offering egg food to both young and adult birds. It is the main food used for rearing young birds and the breeder who uses it can be sure his or her birds will not be lacking in proteins.

Carbohydrates

The second group of macronutrients consists of the carbohydrates, which come in the form of sugars and starches. These also occur in the seeds that you feed to your birds. As sugars are more soluble than starches, the latter are turned into sugar by the action of the enzyme amylase, which occurs in the saliva of the bird. It is then absorbed into the bloodstream, via the small intestine. In the tissues, the sugars are burned up to produce energy and body warmth.

Fats

The final group of macronutrients consists of the fats, which, to a certain extent, perform the same functions as carbohydrates; they are the fuels for warmth and energy in the bird's body. Moreover, they carry vitamins A, D, and E, the latter being the fertility vitamin, which really makes fats essential to the diet. Most fats in the bird's diet are in the form of vegetable oils from the various seeds it eats. The digestion of fats takes longer than carbohydrates, and they are thus useful in the winter when they can help keep the canary fueled-up through the long nights.

Rape seed, canary grass seed, hemp, oats, and flax form the most suitable seed mixture and it is therefore not surprising to learn that these

Average Percentages of Macronutrients in Seeds

Seeds	Protein	Fat	Fiber
Canary grass seed	11.9%	4.5%	10.9%
Rape seed (Holland)	20.4%	43.6%	6.6%
Linseed (flax)	21.5%	35.0%	6.2%
Millet seed			
Red (proso)	11.6%	3.7%	6.8%
Small yellow	12.0%	4.0%	6.8%
White	12.0%	4.1%	8.3%
Niger (black) seed	24.9%	36.2%	17.5%
Hemp	21.4%	35.3%	6.2%
Oats	15.4%	6.3%	2.4%
Sesame seed	22.0%	42.9%	10.3%

Canaries need minerals, especially prior to the breeding season (apricot red-factor male).

seeds play an important role in the diet of your birds. The "oily seeds" mentioned in the table are those that the canaries can receive more of in the winter.

Minerals

Calcium and trace elements are the mineral part of the diet. In combination with phosphorus, calcium, a very important element, is essential for the structure of the bones and for the formation of the eggshell. Trace elements, such as sodium, chlorine, potassium, magnesium, iron, copper, zinc, cobalt, molybdenum, sulphur, iodine, and manganese, are also important but are required only in minute quantities. The absence of even some of these minute quantities of minerals in the diet can cause certain malfunctions in the metabolism.

However, you need not worry too much about the trace elements. There are many good preparations on the market that you can give your birds as a dietary supplement to make sure that they will get all of the essential elements, such as trace mineral salt blocks, grit, cuttlebone, and cooked and crushed eggshell.

Vitamins

Vitamins are organic materials that are found in small quantities in various foodstuffs. They are very important, but the fancier who feeds his or her birds a good seed mixture and fresh greens need not worry too much about them as they will be contained in the food.

A deficiency of one or more important vitamins will result in one of the avitaminosis diseases. After the discovery of the first vitamin (vitamin A), a number of others followed. The most important are A, B, C, D, and E, with vitamin D and especially vitamin B consisting of groups of vitamins.

Vitamin A is necessary for growth; it prevents night blindness and is found in cod-liver oil, green food, germinating seeds, milk, leafy vegetables, orange fruits, and so on.

The vitamin B-complex consists of eight vitamins, most of which are found in yeast, cod-liver oil, liver, milk, lean meat, eggs, vegetables, legumes, corn, bananas, beans, and peanuts. B-complex vitamins help in the digestion of carbohydrates, promote growth, and prevent anemia.

Vitamin C is produced by the bird itself. It also is contained in fresh, leafy greens, oranges, and lemons. Vitamin C fortifies the immune system and thus helps protect against disease. It also plays a major part in the healing of wounds.

Vitamin D is formed in the bird's body in conjunction with the influence of sunlight. It also is contained in cod-liver oil and milk. This vitamin is essential for the healthy development of bones; calcium can be processed in the body only with the help of it.

Vitamin E is found in germinating seeds, especially in wheat germ. It is important for healthy reproduction.

The role that vitamins play in the metabolism of the bird's (or any animal's) body is very important. Vitamin-rich foodstuffs must therefore always be available to your birds. This means fresh, high-quality seeds, fresh green food, germinating seeds, half-ripe weed seeds, and fruits.

As long as canaries receive such a balanced variety, there will be no worries as far as vitamins are concerned. They require only tiny amounts of these various vitamins and these certainly will be present in such a food mixture. There is therefore no necessity to give your birds supplementary cod-liver oil or other vitamin preparations. An exception is when a bird is actually suffering from a vitamin deficiency. Wheat germ oil is sometimes used to increase the ration of vitamin E when infertile eggs are being laid. This vitamin is present

Sprouted seeds. Top: After about five days (left), the first sprouts appear, and after another two days (right) they may be offered to the birds. Bottom: Even after eight to ten days, this fresh green food is very palatable. Always rinse before feeding!

Plastic containers for seed or water should be cleaned at least once a day.

in germinating seeds and green food, so this should not be necessary if the birds are receiving a balanced diet.

If there happens to be a shortage of green foods in the winter, a couple of drops of cod-liver oil or other vitamin preparation can be added to the seed.

Germinating seeds can be given at all times but especially in the winter. To prepare some, soak a little canary seed or wheat in water for an hour, strain, then squeeze out the water, put the seed in a plastic bag, and keep it in a warm place overnight. The seeds will begin to germinate and can then be given to the birds. Some of the damp seeds can be allowed to sprout, providing additional wholesome foodstuffs.

Water

Drinking water is, of course, very important. Canaries should have fresh, clean water available at all times. A canary's muscles are composed of about 75 percent water and there is a lot of water in all other parts of the body. Water is also important in the blood, for excretion, and in the egg. Renew the water at regular set times each day as unclean water can be the source of disease, or the means of transferring diseases from one bird to the next.

The drinking vessel is best made of stainless steel, glass, or porcelain so that it can be cleaned easily and sterilized. The vessel should be so constructed and positioned that the chance of pollution is minimal.

shelter should provide adequate water for your birds in most areas. Filter the water first through charcoal before giving it to your canaries. Better, safer, and rather expensive is bottled drinking water or distilled water for human consumption; it is available everywhere.

In the winter, one must be particularly vigilant as the drinking water can freeze over (it is best to give the water in the night shelter to help prevent this). Also, in the winter, do not provide an open bath of water, as bathing in freezing weather can be very dangerous for canaries.

Normal tap water usually is treated with chlorine and chloramines as a sterilizing agent, and sometimes fluorine is added to help prevent tooth decay for humans. Whether these chemicals are damaging to birds has yet to be proven and, indeed, probably has not been seriously researched. What we do know is that tap water is not good for aquariums and can be fatal to some fish, depending on the amount and nature of the additives. Many fanciers are not so sure about tap water, especially when it comes to young birds, and thus collect rainwater. A 50-gallon (189-L) drum collecting rainwater from the roof of a garden shed or even the aviary night

Practical Canary Feeding

The practice of actually feeding canaries is probably more important than the theoretical aspect. Some fanciers even have made themselves experts in this branch of the hobby.

Treats: In the trade there are all types of treats with which the canary can be "spoiled"—mixtures and tidbits containing all kinds of vitamins, hormones, minerals, wheat germ, and so on. Whoever wants to use such preparations may as well take up a study on enzymes, amino acids, trace elements, and the differences between phosphoric and carbonated calcium.

It is a fact that canary breeders who fuss with all these tonics and pick-me-ups do not necessarily breed better birds than breeders who just make sure that their birds get a balanced diet. Consider the person who eats crisp breads and meat, caviar, and goose liver pâté. He remains alive and well, but this does not mean that he will not suffer later with stomach and gallbladder problems. And he is no healthier than another person who eats wholemeal bread and a vegetable and meat stew. On the contrary, canaries do much better on the usual, healthy diet consisting of rape seed and canary grass seed in a ratio of 40:60. Such fresh, wholesome seeds in the diet will mean no problems with your birds.

Canary food concentrate: Additionally, your birds should get a daily teaspoonful of either universal/condition food or egg food. Conditioning food can be bought but it is quite easy to make up your own formula with the advantage that you will know precisely what's in it. A good recipe for a canary food concentrate is: 4 parts canary grass seed, 5 parts rolled oats, 1 part linseed, 1 part hemp seed, 1 part niger seed, 1 part small yellow millet, 3 parts poppy or maw seed. Salad seed, which is rather expensive, can be left out.

Toward the end of the breeding season, and when it is time to begin preparing your birds for the coming exhibitions, the hemp seed should be left out of this mixture, as it has a darkening effect on the plumage. This can be replaced with a similar amount of small, black sunflower seed or linseed, which will improve the sheen in the plumage.

Seeds of wild plants: In order to enrich the usual menu, the seeds of wild plants can be given when they are in season. The whole seed heads of thistles (Canada and perennial sow), rabbitsfoot grass, Kentucky bluegrass, spear grass, dock, and so on can be offered. The birds will be delighted and will spend all day picking out the seeds. Naturally, the supply should be renewed daily.

Green food: Green food, including chickweed, lettuce, and spinach, (see page 50) can be given daily. Be careful with green food from retail vegetable stands, which may have been sprayed; this is dangerous for your birds. You can grow your own green food from various seeds.

Calcium: One also must make sure that the birds have a regular supply of calcium. This can be given in the form of bird grit (available from avicultural suppliers), or in finely ground, sterilized chicken eggshells or, best of all, cuttlebone.

The best method of supplying calcium is with a cuttlebone.

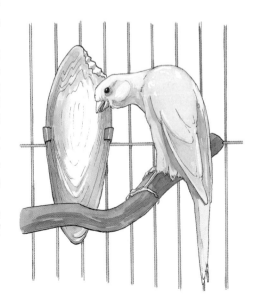

Egg Food or Rearing Food

There is nothing in the canary fancy that has been so experimented with, indeed "messed around" with, as egg food. Egg is an important source of animal protein for canaries, and egg food is therefore a very useful addition to the food of developing youngsters.

In practice it has been shown that egg food has been misused by fanciers who believe that they can make a formula better or cheaper than a purchased one. Egg food is best given fresh each day. It is available on the market but some breeders make up an amount every day, or make up enough to last a few days or even for a few weeks.

There is no problem with commercially supplied egg food; in most cases it is expertly and carefully put together. But canaries would rather have egg food that can be made from a mixture of a hard-boiled egg with four rusks. The so-called egg bread or canary biscuits that are available are not as good. Mixtures containing dried egg powder are even less impressive,

The best kind of egg food is made from an egg that has been boiled for ten minutes, mashed as finely as possible, then mixed with crushed rusks or unseasoned bread crumbs. A few poppy seeds, lettuce seeds, or some finely chopped chickweed will make the mixture even more nutritious. A tiny (knife point) of sodium bicarbonate is added to the mixture by some breeders as it tends to aid the birds' digestion. However, this is not strictly necessary unless you think the birds are having digestion problems.

Egg food should always be given *fresh*. This is extremely important during breeding. Old egg food gets stale, sour, and dry and the birds no longer want it. They may even stop feeding their young.

Some breeders use bread crumbs obtained from white or wholemeal bread—make sure it is not moldy. The bread is placed in the sun or in a low-temperature oven until it is hard and dry. It can then be reduced easily to fine crumbs with a rolling pin, in a food grinder, or mashed with a fork, before being mixed with the finely ground, hard-boiled egg.

Egg food should be given to those birds you wish to breed with, well before the breeding season starts, so that it is not given suddenly when they start to breed. Newly fledged canaries also require an ongoing supply of egg food, as they are still developing and will need to *gradually* change over to a normal adult canary diet.

Green Food

A canary in a cage should be given green food at least once, preferably twice a week. It can be given a lettuce leaf, some spinach, watercress, dandelion leaves, shepherd's purse, or chickweed. Most birds like a piece of carrot. The ideal of course, would be to offer a small amount of green food daily. All greens should be fresh and crisp and any left over at bedtime should be removed and discarded. In order to offer safe, unsprayed greens it is good to grow your own, if you have the time and/or the space. Bought greens should be washed thoroughly in cold, clean water before being offered to the birds.

Fruit

Most canaries will take fruit in one form or another. They will pick eagerly at pieces of sweet apple, pear, pineapple, cherries, plums, peaches, melon, grapes, tomatoes, and grapefruit. Large pieces of fruit are best impaled on a nail that has been driven into a piece of wood—in the aviary you can have one or two nails in the framework especially for this purpose— so that the fruit does not become soiled on the floor. Fruit also could be placed in a small wire basket that is hung on the cage wire.

Treats

A number of very good treats for canaries can be obtained in the pet stores; these include seed mixtures with various dehydrated fruits and vegetables, egg, nuts, animal proteins, and so on. These aid as a pick-me-up and help condition the bird after breeding, molting, and so on. Such treats may be given in addition to the normal diet, but in a separate container. Pieces of fruit, freshly grated carrot, honey sticks—and variations such as egg stick, fruit stick, and veggie stick—and similar items are all regarded as treats. Be careful with bread, cake, and cookies, as these will make the bird fat, and a fat bird is not a healthy one.

If a bird is off color, or when a hen is rearing young, a little bread soaked in low-fat milk can be given. Boil the milk first and pour it over a

Canaries require greens, especially in the breeding season. These include (left to right): shepherd's purse, dandelion, watercress, and chickweed.

Feeding time!

piece of stale wholemeal bread. A little poppy seed sprinkled over this will encourage a bird to try it.

Color Feeding

To achieve a purity and depth of tone in the plumage, certain canary varieties are given the so-called color foods during the molt. However, this does not mean that poorly colored birds can be drastically improved by color feeding.

The canary varieties that usually are color fed include the red-factor, the lizard, the Norwich, and the Yorkshire.

Color feeding is a practice that goes back to about 1870 when cayenne pepper was first mixed with the seed. This practice was soon changed when it was discovered that sweet red pepper had a better effect; even today, fanciers quite often mix this into the canaries' soft food. In recent years, canthaxanthin has been used. This is derived from cantharel, an edible fungus that seems to have no vitamin value. It works in other organisms including some insects, fish, and flamingo and scarlet ibis feathers. Pure canthaxanthin is used in a dosage of 0.05–0.1 grams per pound (500 g) to intensify and hold the red color in the plumage.

We usually administer this color food via crumbly, moist egg or soft food and begin a week before the molt. Young birds get color food at about eight weeks of age. There are various other color foods available on the market; these should be used as per the manufacturer's instructions.

Conditioning or Universal Food

In addition to eggs and bread crumbs, this soft food contains various seeds, such as dandelion, thistle, maw or poppy seed, lettuce, some hemp, linseed, teasel, and niger seed. This kind of food—obtainable under various brand names—should be offered in small glass, stainless steel, or porcelain containers, two or three times a week throughout the year. It acts as a tonic for show or breeding birds especially, and helps bring birds into top condition after the molt. Personally, we give our birds the opportunity to take this food daily throughout the fall and winter months. As this food is likely to spoil quickly, especially in warm weather, leftovers must be removed and disposed of in the evening. Always use it sparingly and place the container in a shady spot that is easy to reach by the birds. In aviaries with several birds, two or more containers should be placed in different spots, so that all birds get the chance to feed in peace.

Pellets/Extruded Diets

Only approximately eight percent of all canary fanciers buy single-particle diets, whereas 75 percent of all bird owners still rely on seed as the mainstay of their pet birds' diet.

Extruded diets are not new to the pet industry, but they are the diet alternative for cage and aviary birds. They look similar to standard pelleted diets, but looks are deceiving. Pelleting is a completely different process than extrusion, however. In the pelleting process, dry ground-up nutrients are compressed into a pellet, which is heated up to 190°F (88°C). During extrusion, on the other hand, wet ingredients are combined into a soupy mixture, which is subjected to approximately 25 different atmospheric pressures and temperatures up to 320°F (179°C). A pellet's inner core become insulated during compression and may not reach 171°F (77°C), the temperature needed to kill salmonella and pseudomonas viruses. Extrusion, however, is the most bacteriologically safe method of formulating a diet, and it makes the food the most digestible to the end user. The wet process also allows manufacturers to form different shapes and textures that appeal to birds' natural curiosity and make the diet more readily acceptable. Because the ingredients already are broken down, extruded diets offer greater digestibility.

The main benefit of a single particle is that it can include all the ingredients necessary to sustain a bird. Pellets contain readily digestible ingredients, and offer balanced ratios of vitamins, minerals, and amino acids, without supplementation. Single-particle diets are also more economical because they result in less waste.

The biggest controversy over pellets and extruded diets concerns protein content. More avian nutritionists agree that a bird's diet should consist of no more than 16 percent protein, but many pelleted and extruded diets contain more protein than that. The link between higher protein levels and gout can be attributed to the fact that most birds won't eat at first when switched to pellets or extruded diets, raising their nitrogen levels. Higher nitrogen levels lead to gout.

One well-known brand was even used as a hand-feeding diet in lovebirds and blue-crowned conures. The young birds developed external signs of gout, according to Richard R. Ney, DVM, with "urate deposits around the tendon sheaths of the lower legs and around the joints. Internal lesions involved urates on the serosal surfaces of the liver, spleen, intestine, and the pericardial sac. The kidneys were grossly enlarged and the tubules were dilated and congested with urates. A similar scenario presented itself in an aviary of lovebirds where only the adults were fed the pelleted diet and they, in turn, fed the young. In cockatiels I've seen several cases of polydipsia/polyuria related to (the used) diet, and chemistries revealed elevated blood uric acid levels greater than 16 mg/dl." (*Journal of the Association of Avian Veterinarians*, Volume 3, No. 4, Winter, 1989.)

Getting canaries to eat a different type of food, given their fears and finicky nature, can be a tricky business. A canary or any other bird that has spent its whole life feeding on a diet consisting largely of seeds is not likely to become suddenly enthusiastic about pellets or an extruded diet. Converting a bird to such a change in diet sometimes can be a difficult task also, and may require much patience. The best method for canaries is to give them a 1–9 ratio, meaning 10 percent pellets or extruded diet and 90 percent seeds. Each day for the next 10 days, add 10 percent more pellets or extruded diet to the mixture. At the end of the 10 days, the diet will consist of 100 percent pellets or extruded diet. During the transition period, watch for a change in the consistency of droppings, a "fluffed-up" or sleepy appearance, and a constant search for food. If these symptoms persist for more than 24 hours, consult an avian veterinarian immediately and reinstate the former diet.

Personally, we think canaries always should have access to fresh green food, germinated seeds, fruits, and various seeds as well as small pellets or an extruded crumble.

Chapter Four

Canary Breeding

It is easy to breed canaries, in fact, so simple that it is difficult to believe that anything could go wrong. How often do you hear of beginners who, with no specialized knowledge other than a little advice from a dealer, raise several broods of faultless youngsters? Practically all canary fanciers are aware of such examples of beginner's luck, but they shrug their shoulders with the knowledge that things do not always turn out so successfully.

But the many examples of beginner's luck show us that canary breeding is not a complicated matter. A good breeding pair of canaries will raise a brood in the breeding season anyway, beginner's luck or not; and this example can be followed by almost any breeding pair. Beginners are normally contented with a simple pair of yellow, green, or variegated canaries and are not bothered with the problems of rearing the "racehorses" of the canary fancy that, through inbreeding and hybridizing, concern the serious canary breeder.

The beginner usually starts modestly with a pair and, with the ardor of a beginner, cares for the birds by giving them all of his or her free time. This care is rewarded by the birds in the first season.

"Ah," the beginner thinks, "it goes like that—16 youngsters from one pair, that is, 160 young from ten pairs. I'll show the canary fanciers something!"

So in the following season the fancier breeds with 10 pairs; he or she takes the same amount of care, but his or her estimates are proven wrong.

They would be even more wrong if the fancier would start with red-factor canaries. It is not because not

A clutch of canary eggs.

Two- and three-day-old non-frosted yellow chicks with their parents.

desired goal is reached. And it still can happen that one knows a trick too few.

Therefore, numbers of difficulties for all aspiring breeders of canaries in each breeding season can be predicted. These are the difficulties with which every serious canary breeder has to contend. But without these difficulties, the canary fancy would not be what it is today. If it were so easy, would it be so challenging? The ups and downs, the striving for success, the overcoming of difficulties, the alternating luck and misfortune, the surprising, the difficult, and so on, make the canary fancy a hobby that means a great deal to its participants.

all cocks are good fathers or not all hens are good mothers. It is not because the breeder is not an experienced breeder who feeds too much or wrongly. It is not because he or she buys the wrong birds from the wrong people, or that his or her hens feed the young badly, or that many eggs are infertile. It is not because the weather was too wet or too cold, or because disease broke out, or so on and so forth.

This may sound somewhat discouraging, but the reality is that canary breeding as a hobby is not always the delight that one expects. Indeed, the reality is quite different from the theory; canary breeding can be easy *or* difficult. It is easy if one is lucky, and it frequently turns out to be very difficult at the moment one thinks the techniques have been mastered.

The more one learns about canaries the better; one needs to learn a thousand tricks before the

Canary Breeding Techniques

Canary breeding can take on various forms. The breeder has different names for these different methods:

• *monogamous breeding*—one cock and one hen are put together in a breeding cage and allowed to rear their broods;

• *polygamous breeding*—one cock serves several hens. The cock is used for fertilization only and, after each mating is moved to another cage with another hen. Frequently, a cock may be used with three or more hens that must brood and rear the young by themselves;

• *colony breeding*—a number of cocks and hens are placed in an aviary and allowed to breed as they wish. In this system, two or more hens per cock also are used frequently.

Let's take a closer look at each of these systems.

Monogamous breeding has many advantages. If you have a good breeding pair, then success is almost ensured. With a stable pair, the cock will help to feed the young, which lightens the hen's work load and ensures rapid growth and satisfactory development of the young. If such a mating should be unsuccessful, then it is easy to find out what was wrong and to take steps to correct the failing.

The system is technically simple and it is easy to know the ancestry of the young and thus what genetic factors are entailed, information that may be very useful in future seasons. One disadvantage of the system is that it can be more expensive, in that each breeding cage is taken up with a single pair.

Polygamous breeding is used by most serious breeders as it has many advantages, but the system also has disadvantages that cannot be ignored. The most usual combination is one cock to three hens; thus, 30 breeding hens require 10 cocks. This means, of course, that the breeder needs to keep fewer cocks for next season's breeding, allowing him or her to sell more and, if they are good quality, to boost the returns. A further advantage of the system is that the breeder can be much more selective, the 10 breeding cocks will be of the highest quality and there will be some good male offspring from which to select. Moreover, a smaller number of cocks will

Twelve-day-old non-frosted yellow chicks in nest at right.

mean fewer mouths to feed, especially during the unproductive winter season.

The disadvantages of this system include the fact that during the breeding season, the cocks must be transferred from one breeding cage to another in order to fertilize another hen, and, to keep each visit to each hen as short as possible, the breeder must continually stay by his or her birds.

The system also requires reliable hens, capable of rearing a brood on their own. Every hen is not necessarily reliable in such cases, and those that may have been perfect mothers in partnership with a cock may turn out to be totally unreliable with enforced single-parenthood.

With this method, it is also easy to keep a studbook, as the breeder knows the mother and father of each brood. Another advantage is that the number of young per cock is greater than in the monogamous system.

The colony system is the easiest system as all birds are placed together in an aviary. The breeder has thus just one cage to keep clean, feeding and watering is simpler, and less control is necessary. With this system, one also can use fewer cocks, usually one cock to three hens.

The biggest disadvantage of the colony system is that one cannot be sure which young are from which parents. It is possible for four young in a nest, for example, each to have been sired by a different father, and one cannot be sure that mothers are always brooding their own eggs and young.

In practice, this system is really useful only for those who wish to breed numbers of canaries for sheer pleasure and not worry about the ancestry of the young. For the serious breeder, this system is used only if he or she requires birds of a particular color, and uses only parents with the correct genetical factors, for example, only white, only frosted ivory, gold, silver, brown, apricot, and so on.

The Breeding Season

Normally, the breeding season starts for all birds in the spring. It is controlled by hormones, glandular secretions, and metabolic changes in the birds' bodies. It is a well-known fact that the photoperiod (length of daylight) and temperature increases play an important part in preparing animals to breed. The sun begins to shine for longer periods in the spring; the days become longer. As the birds receive more sunshine, the glands begin to work hard, preparing the bird's body for the tough times ahead and sparking off the urge to mate and breed.

In northern temperate areas, the urge to breed is at its most intense in April and May, so that is the time to start breeding your canaries. However, canaries are so domesticated, you can bend the rules just a little, if necessary.

Experienced breeders can bring their birds into breeding condition in January by exposing them to longer periods of artificial light. The question of whether this is a good thing to do has never been answered satisfactorily. Imperfect birds seem to be more common among those bred early in the season, and some breeders seem to think that many canary parents today are not as good as they were at one time.

It is desirable that the breeder is aware of the phenomena that indicate the birds' readiness to start breeding.

• Both cock and hen will show increased restlessness as they begin to come into breeding condition. They will begin to take more interest in the opposite sex.

• The cock's song becomes stronger and keener and, as his condition reaches its high point, somewhat hoarser.

• The interest between sexes increases and minor battles between cocks will take place over particular hens. There is no need to worry about this as it is a natural process.

Condition

At breeding time, each pair of birds should be in top condition; if not, perhaps it is too early in the season, or one or more of the birds is not ready for some other reason. In the first case, the breeder must have a little

patience; in the second case, the "defective" bird is not used for breeding. Experience will show that one has to be quite ruthless in making such decisions. If you hang onto these problems, they will persist and it is thus best to get rid of them at the outset.

Age

If one of a pair shows a deficiency in the breeding urge, it frequently is a result of its age. Success is unlikely if birds are used when they are too young—infertile eggs, abandoned eggs or nestlings, bad feeding of the nestlings, and so on will be common.

A breeding canary should be at least nine months old; ten months is even better. In practice, this means that birds from only the first brood of the one season can be used for breeding in the next. Canaries born at the beginning of July are not sexually mature until late March in the following year, and thus are not ready for breeders who like to start their birds off in January or February.

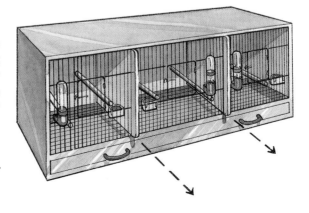

The "triple-breeder" has a center compartment that is used when pairing one cock with two hens.

Breeding Cages and Nesting Facilities

The serious breeder of canaries usually uses single and double breeding cages. The single breeding cage is usually 16 inches (40 cm) long, 12 inches (30 cm) high, and 14 inches (35 cm) deep. The double cage is the same height and depth but twice as long, with a sliding partition in the middle dividing it into two singles.

The nests can be placed inside the cages, but they will decrease the interior space. It is recommended that they be placed outside the cages (two per cage—necessary in case the hen starts on her second brood before the first has fledged) with access through an opening in the cage wall. These nests have the advantage of being easier to inspect than those inside the cage.

Non-frosted green canary hen on her nest.

A Separate Chamber

Even better than the usual single or double breeding cage is one with a separate chamber where the cock and later the young can be housed separately. With a double cage, such a chamber can be arranged between the two breeding cages. In this chamber, there are two sliding hatches giving entrance to the breeding cages.

Such a joint chamber has many uses in monogamous and polygamous breeding. With the polygamous system, one cock is used with several hens. One naturally can use the single breeding cage for this system and catch the cock after he has fertilized the hen and put him in with another hen. It is easier and better, however, to use a double breeding cage and better still, one with a chamber in between the two.

Close the popholes between the cages and chamber with a piece of sliding hardboard or plywood. Place the cock in the central chamber. As soon as one of the hens starts playing with nest material, open the pophole so that the cock can reach the hen. As soon as he has fertilized the hen, shut him back in the chamber, ready to fertilize the other hen.

The great advantage of this system is that the breeding hen is not disturbed. The cock can be caught easily in his chamber and used in another similar double setup. The chamber has another advantage: As the young get bigger, but not quite independent,

Canary breeding cages.

the hen could start to pluck them for nest material for the next brood. This can be prevented by providing a bunch of chicken feathers in the breeding cage, but the best way is to put the young in the chamber and replace the slide with wire so that the hen still can feed them but not pluck them.

Yet another advantage of such a cage is that when the young are fledged, the partitions can be removed to make a long flight cage for the young.

Cage Material

How or from what the cages are made does not really matter. One can purchase breeding cages from avicultural suppliers, but these are usually expensive and you can make your own quite easily. The best and easiest materials to use are wood, thin solid lumber, or hardboard. During construction, make sure that not too many nooks and crannies are left for mites, lice, and other pests to harbor themselves. The front of the cage is made of a sturdy wire. These cage fronts can be purchased quite cheaply and the cages can be made to fit them. The wire fronts are furnished with a sliding door and openings for food and water hoppers. The openings in the ends of the cages are slightly smaller than the entrances to the nest boxes, which are suspended over the openings with hooks and eyes.

Perches

Each breeding cage has four perches—two up and two down.

Two-day-old red-orange chicks.

Three-day-old non-frosted green chicks.

The two lower ones should be about 6 inches (15 cm) apart and situated so that the birds can easily reach food and water hoppers from them. The upper perches are affixed at either end of the cage, about 3 inches (7.5 cm) from the walls.

Nest Pans

If nest pans are placed inside the cage, they are usually fixed to the rear wall between the two perches. Special ceramic, wood, or wire gauze nests can be used; the latter, made from galvanized mesh, are the best and will last for many years.

Nest Boxes and Material

Nest boxes also are available from specialist suppliers, but it is quite easy to make your own. These are usually 6 × 6 × 8 inches (15 × 15 × 20 cm) with the nest part about an inch (a few centimeters) deep. A hollow in the base is lined with nest material.

The best nest materials are sisal fibers and unraveled sisal string cut into lengths of about 2 inches (5 cm). This material is soft enough and allows good ventilation through the fibers, and the canaries like the light color of it. There is no better known nest material. The flax that can be bought in avicultural stores looks ideal, but is clings together in a felty mass and the bird could get its claws caught in it or worst, could hang itself. This also can happen with the young. You could cut the flax shorter, but you may miss a few threads.

Some breeders use cotton threads, dried grass, moss, or coconut fibers, all cut into short lengths.

Many breeders swear by the material they use; each convinced that theirs is the best, but one thing is certain: Hens prefer lighter-colored materials over darker ones. You can also buy preformed nest platforms made of sisal fibers or coarse felt.

Tray

In the bottom of the cage, fit a sliding tray. Place a layer of ground corncob bedding, bird sand, or clean river sand in this and change it at regular intervals. Always use clean, dry sand; you can wash it yourself by placing it in a bucket or similar container and swirling a current of water through it from a hose until the effluent runs clear. Then spread the clean sand on a clean flat surface and allow it to dry in the sun.

Accessories

Food and water hoppers are attached to the front of the cage over the special openings. They are perhaps not very attractive but they are hygienic and functional. It is easy to inspect the contents of the hoppers and to quickly clean and refill them, an advantage for the busy breeder with many cages to maintain.

A less important accessory is a rack for nest material, which can be attached to the wire front. Such a rack also can be used for green food, which otherwise would be dragged about in the dirt on the cage floor.

Canaries also can be bred in an aviary using plastic or ceramic pans, or wire nests, also small Harz cages.

In the latter, the birds feel safer and can brood more peacefully as they are not so readily disturbed.

Number of Birds

In the aviary you can use up to four hens per cock, or, for example, three cocks to ten hens. The advantage of this method is that there is less work, but there are some disadvantages, especially if other birds are in the aviary and there is a chance of losing a brood through disturbances. Another disadvantage is that one cannot be sure of the ancestry of any of the youngsters, as any cock in the aviary could be the father of any of the young. It is therefore not good for the selective breeder of canaries; it is, however, good for the breeder with little free time who does not care what colors are produced.

Artificial canary eggs.

63

The Beginning of the Breeding Process

Once the cages are ready, breeding can begin.

1. The hen is usually placed in the breeding cage first, the cock introduced a couple of days later. In the meantime, he can be housed in a small separate cage next to the breeding cage; he will show his readiness to breed by singing heartily. If he does not do this, then he is not ready to mate. Either replace him with another cock or be patient for a few more days.

2. It will not take long for the hen to survey the breeding cage and inspect the nesting pans. She will take some nest material in her beak and bring it to the chosen nest. This is the signal for most breeders to place the cock in the breeding cage with the hen.

3. The birds usually don't hit it off right away, but the experienced breeder knows this is natural and does not worry himself over these little pairing squabbles as long as they don't get out of hand. When the squabbles are over, the pair works feverishly to build the nest. The cock often brings the materials while the hen fashions the nest to her liking. It is at this time that the hen starts sitting and making a noise inviting the cock to mate with her.

4. The first egg soon appears in the nest, usually followed by a second, third, and fourth in the next days. The hen spends a lot of time at the nest from the first day, but serious incubating usually does not start until the third day so that the eggs will all hatch in a short period of time. Some breeders replace the

A little self-made cabinet to store canary eggs until the clutch is complete.

first eggs with artificial ones and put all the real eggs back on the fourth day, but this is unnecessary and one should allow nature to take its own course.

Although the average clutch consists of four eggs, there are hens that lay two or three, and others that lay as many as six.

5. As the hen incubates, the cock, like a good husband, stays near her, singing her a song, but otherwise leaving her in peace. If he does not, then he should be removed from the breeding cage and the hen left to rear the brood on her own.

Food

Food given during this time should consist of rape seed and egg food (the latter so that the birds get used to it and will later feed egg food to their young), also calcium—finely ground eggshells—and daily green food. But other kinds of seeds and universal food are not given.

Candling

The eggs often are examined—this is called "candling"—during the first five days to see if they are fertile. Candling, or holding an egg in front of a strong light, is the best way to test it for fertility. We have constructed a candling box with a compartment for the egg on top and a socket for a 40-watt bulb below. The egg compartment has a floor made of narrow-mesh woolen netting. We have seen ordinary hairnets used successfully the same way. The important thing is to have a net soft enough to prevent cracking and a mesh narrow enough to keep the eggs from falling through. There are also portable transilluminators commercially available that feature a high-intensity, prefocused bulb on the end or an approximately 10-inch (25-cm) flexible shaft that can be bent into any configuration.

A cursory look can distinguish fertilized eggs from unfertilized eggs; the lamp light will show you the embryo in the fertile ones. You can see movements—the beginning of life—but don't get carried away by watching the miracle of life because the intense heat of the light bulb isn't good for the embryo; too much exposure would kill it. And don't candle the eggs more than once.

If you wait longer than eight days you don't need to candle to check eggs of your canaries. You don't even have to pick them up. Infertile eggs look pale red ("dirty red," some fanciers say); fertilized eggs, in contrast, can be distinguished starting about five days after the onset of brooding (incubating), by their purplish brown, shiny tint.

If the eggs are fertile, you soon will find out on the thirteenth day when they should start to hatch. Infertile eggs can, of course, be removed from the nest but it its really better to leave them all there as the infertile eggs act as support for the young when they hatch. If all eggs are infertile, take the nest away. Let the hen rest for a week and then let her try again. Moving perches can cause infertile eggs.

Feeding Techniques

• Add warm (100–110°F [38–43°]) bottled (not distilled) water or apple juice to the formula.

• Mix formula well until it has the consistency of creamy milk. Never have the formula too thick because it will congeal in the crop and will be unable to pass into the stomach. By giving the bird lukewarm water and some gentle crop massaging, this problem can be easily corrected. If, however, the crop remains full or is not emptying correctly, there could be a digestive problem. Consult an avian veterinarian or an experienced bird breeder immediately.

• Draw formula into a plastic eye-dropper or syringe or let it roll off a teaspoon, the sides of which have been bent inward—the feeding tool we like best. The feeding utensil should be as close to the temperature of the formula as possible: 100–110°F (38–43°C).

• Use one feeding instrument and one feeding dish per bird. Never dip a feeding instrument into the food dish of another bird after it has touched the first bird's mouth. Sterilize your feeding instrument after every feeding.

• Maintain the right temperature for the formula during the whole feeding process by placing the dish with bird formula in a pan of warm (100–110°F [38–43°C]) water.

• Place the bird on a flat surface on a bath towel that feels warm to the touch.

• When a baby bird doesn't want to open its beak (gape), tap it gently on the beak with the feeding utensil. This will encourage the baby bird to gape (or pump).

• Examine the bird's crop before feeding to determine the frequency and volume of the feeding. Remember, a crop should never become completely empty. Usually the crop will empty itself in three and a half to four hours.

• Don't overfill the crop. Overfilling can lead to backflow up the gullet (esophagus), into the throat, and down the windpipe, and kill the bird.

• Always determine the fullness of the bird's crop. Stop feeding immediately when the food is flowing back

Hand-feeding baby canaries.

into the mouth. Don't resume feeding until the mouth is completely empty again.

• Feeding has to be synchronized with swallowing. As soon as the baby bird swallows, which goes with a rhythmic bobbing of the head, deliver the formula quickly. Place the feeding device into the mouth over the tongue.

• Support the bird while feeding, with a cupped (and warm) hand.

• After each feeding, rinse the bird's mouth with a few drops of warm (100–110°F [38–43°C]) water.

• After each feeding, clean the bird's beak, head, and other body parts, including the anus (vent), with lukewarm water and return the bird to its warm (90–95°F [32–35°C]) quarters.

Hatching to one week: A baby canary can be taken from its parents after 10 to 12 days, or when the chick is just starting to feather, the later, the safer. However, when you must hand-feed a hatchling, note the following: Don't feed a hatchling for the first 10 to 15 hours, then start with one drop of lukewarm water. After one hour, feed another drop, thereafter, a few drops of very thin formula every hour around the clock.

One to two weeks: Feed every two to three hours around the clock. If the birds are properly housed (warm and comfortable, at a temperature of 90–95°F [32–35°C]), feeding after midnight can be eliminated until 5:00 A.M. The formula must now

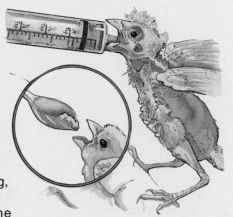

To hand feed young canaries, use a syringe, plastic eyedropper, or a teaspoon with its sides bent inward.

have the consistency of light cream.

Two to three weeks: Feed every three to four hours from 5:00 A.M. to midnight. Continue a formula consistency of light cream.

Three to four weeks: Feed every four hours with a slightly thicker formula that has a consistency of heavy cream. Birds must be housed in a cage with low perches and a shallow bowl of water.

Five to six weeks: Feed a formula with the consistency of light cream. Introduce free choice of sprouted seeds and millet spray, or whatever is required to encourage the baby bird to forage on its own. Mix some formula with the food.

Seven to eight weeks: Feed the formula once a day. House the baby bird in a large cage with proper food cups and water bowl.

Three 10-day-old steel-blue x non-frosted green chicks, and one non-frosted green youngster.

Ten-day-old red-orange chicks. Note the way the hen has arranged the youngsters' droppings!

Incubation, Hatching, and Rearing

The incubation time for canary eggs is 13 days. Incubation does not usually start until the third egg has been laid. In this way, the canary itself makes sure that the young all hatch in a fairly short period of time, usually all on the same day. After laying the first egg, the hen will spend a lot of time in the nest, but serious incubation will not start until after the third egg.

A good hen will brood diligently for the 13 days of incubation time. She does not often leave the nest and, in a good canary marriage, she is fed by the cock in the nest. It is recommended that during incubation, things are not allowed to get too dry, as dryness can stop the eggs

from hatching smoothly. Make sure that bathwater is always available; it will do no harm for the incubating hen to take a quick bath. It will indeed help to keep the all-important humidity up around the eggs. In very dry conditions, it may help to give a fine mist spray in the cage each day.

Development

Development of the embryo takes place during incubation, and if the eggs are fertile, and all goes well for 13 days, four or five tiny, near-naked canary chicks will hatch. These help-less little mites, nevertheless, have the urge to eat and grow. If some of the eggs fail to hatch, it is good to leave them in the nest for a few days to help support the youngsters that use a lot of energy stretching out their necks and begging for food. At this time, freshly made egg food should be given, softened with a little water.

The egg food should be replaced several times a day in hot weather as it quickly becomes sour and could cause digestive disturbances. With a good feeding hen, the young will grow quickly and strongly and they will always have well-filled crops. One should watch at this stage that crops are indeed full. If not, it can be due to a bad feeding hen. The young can be saved by transferring them to a better foster mother, or they can be hand-reared using Neo-Nate (L/M Animal Farms/Hartz Mountain) or other similar hand-feeding formulas (Nutri-Start [Lafeber Company]; SunDiet [Sun Seed Company]; L'Avian Plus [D & D Commodities]; T.L.C. [Higgins]; Exact [Kaytee]) and various others.

If all goes well, the young grow quickly and soon begin to get feathers. If the cock helps with the feeding, it goes even faster and the nest hollow is soon filled with four or five sturdy, feathered youngsters.

Then real danger threatens, especially by breeders left unheated or in an outdoor aviary.

If the first brood is born in the middle of April, it can be especially cold at night in some parts of the United States. Night frost even can occur in May. If the hen no longer sits on the nest because she thinks the young do not need her, the young can get too cold, especially if there are too few to keep each other warm. A ceramic heat lamp placed near the nest can help prevent this.

If all goes well, the young will be sitting on the edge of the nest at 14 days and it will not be long before they are flying. The parents will continue to feed them for a time but they soon will start picking at the food themselves and it will not be long before they are standing on their own two legs.

Kept in this proper manner, the birds will grow fully with no problems. You must see only that the changeover from rearing food to seed is not too quick. Continue giving a little egg food and also some softened seed until the young gradually get used to it. A little warm water placed on the seeds, drained, and left overnight will soften them for the next day.

Naturally, fresh green food always must be available, one can give them a little carrot to nibble at or, later in the season, a piece of apple.

Eleven-day-old non-frosted yellow chicks.

Twelve-day-old non-frosted yellow chicks.

When the young start to fly, the mother is usually starting her next clutch. You should, of course, supply a second nest so that the following family can be raised in choice surroundings.

Problem Hens

Before the breeding season, canary fanciers must do all they can to make sure that their birds reach top condition, and should provide them with all they need. This includes providing a proper diet, clean drinking and bathing water, proper cages, good nesting facilities and nest material. The rest can be left to nature.

But if nature lets them down, canary fanciers should try to find the cause, so that preventive measures will stop it from happening again. The problem could be a too cold or wet beginning to the season, but this can be avoided by using heat in the bird room.

There can be other reasons for failure. The birds themselves can let the canary fancier down; they might be only mediocre parents, many eggs could be infertile, hens may abandon the eggs, hens may not feed their young properly, and so on.

These all seem to be phenomena that one cannot do much about; you cannot make a canary do things! But sometimes these things can be one's own fault, as the breeding of birds, in general, and canaries, in particular, is dependent on more factors than just their outward welfare.

First, infertile eggs can be the fault of the cock as much as the hen. Many canary breeders, especially those who hope to earn a little money on the side, tend to look upon cocks with different eyes than they do the hens. Cocks bring in more money than hens, so cocks get more attention. The cocks get a better diet; the hens have to make do with a mediocre one. The latter get enough to stay alive, but not much more.

Good canary breeders treat cocks and hens in the same way, so that all birds are in top condition for the breeding season. To improve the possibilities of fertilization:
• Pull away some of the feathers from around the vent of cocks and

hens prior to breeding. This is especially desirable with the thickly plumaged frosted birds. Do not clip feathers as the stubs can hinder pairing or can damage eggs.

• Clip the toenails of the birds; the cocks can thus get a better grip when pairing. Hold the toe against the light and clip just under the visible red blood vessel (quick). It is best to use clippers rather than scissors. The nail then can be filed gently to a point.

• In the last months before the breeding season, provide a regular supply of green food, as vitamins play a big role in fertilization. It is wrong to think that short-term administration of vitamin E (wheat germ oil) will influence the fertilization. It is much more important to see that the birds get vitamin-rich foods all the time. The supplementary feeding of fertility vitamins is then unnecessary.

• The age of breeding birds is at least nine months or preferably older, if possible. Breeding with younger birds is asking for trouble.

• With regard to cocks, select those that show obvious sexual characteristics at the vent. Cocks that do not sing, or those questionable of really being cocks, are best not used!

• The hens should be selected carefully. Hens that did not perform well in the previous season are best left out of your plans. Hens that came from a small nest and were brought up by the skin of their teeth seldom make good mothers. It has not been proven that good brooding and rearing is inherited, but do not ignore the possibility that the young of bad brooders and rearers will themselves be inferior parents. Why take the risk?

• It is therefore important to keep a studbook where all pertinent information on every bird should be recorded. The birds are all leg banded so one can identify every individual and look into its past: its date of birth, its parents, the nest in which it was born, illnesses, and so on—all sorts of information that will indicate if it is going to make a good parent.

With the help of the studbook, the canary fancier can decide which birds to use and not to use for breeding, for example, those that had a digestive or respiratory problem during the winter should not be used.

• Another danger exists in attempting to breed a particular good-colored bird, which could possibly produce good-colored young, but in which success is at least very doubtful. A bird that is outwardly pretty-colored but possesses other inherited factors that would make it a bad parent is unsuitable for breeding, however pretty it may be. Anyone who tries to breed such a bird will have problems; that is indisputable. In this case it is best to choose another partner that will produce less pretty young but will be better breeding birds.

Canaries bred much better at one time than they do today, that is, when color breeding was something new and most canaries were bred for their song. No statistics exist on the similarities or differences in the breeding of color or song canaries. Presumably, such statistics would show that song canaries do breed better than color canaries, as all color canaries with the red factor, for example, have hybrid blood in them. Through hybridization, the canary lost part of its characteristics; it gained other characteristics from the black-hooded red siskin, but definitely not characteristics that would improve its breeding prowess. The breeder must contend with this fact and great care must be taken in the selection of breeding pairs in order to get the very best results.

Leg Banding

Leg banding or ringing is important if you wish to keep a studbook and be able to identify each individual bird, especially if you have a lot of them. If you don't use leg bands, it is surprising how easy it is to forget which bird is which. Canary young are leg banded between seven and nine days of age. Small, closed metal rings are available from avicultural suppliers or societies and can be printed with the personal number of the breeder, the canary number, and the year. Anodized rings are the best; the diameter for canaries is about 7/64 inch (2.9 mm).

To apply a ring, push the first three toes through, then pass it over the hind toe, which is laid back along the leg. This must not be done much later than nine days after hatching: otherwise, it may become difficult or even impossible to do.

In the trade, it is also possible to buy the so-called "open" rings. They may be made of aluminum or plastic and are opened out to place

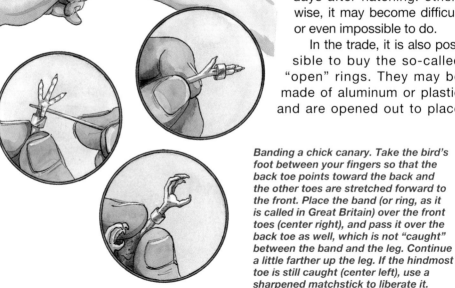

Banding a chick canary. Take the bird's foot between your fingers so that the back toe points toward the back and the other toes are stretched forward to the front. Place the band (or ring, as it is called in Great Britain) over the front toes (center right), and pass it over the back toe as well, which is not "caught" between the band and the leg. Continue a little farther up the leg. If the hindmost toe is still caught (center left), use a sharpened matchstick to liberate it.

around the leg, after which they spring back together. These are useful for ringing older or adult canaries. They can be obtained in various colors, so you can identify, for example, which bird is from which brood, without having to catch it.

Selection

It is important to select carefully. Selection is something that never really stops. Circumstances can change from bird to bird and brood to brood. With the combined knowledge of observation and the studbook, a good impression of suitable breeding birds can be obtained.

Selection begins with the young in the nest as soon as they have been leg banded. The fast developers should be noted as well as the performances of the parents. You should note with which combinations the best young were produced, and, with these first selections, you can prepare the basis of the next breeding season. When the young have fledged, then the experienced eye will be able to pick out the best of the bunch, using these birds in the next show season.

In the months following the breeding season, the decision must be made as to which birds are to be kept for further breeding and which are to be sold. And here there naturally will be an understandable self-interest.

Another, very important selection, will be at the shows. Here the birds

Note the band (ring) around this champion frosted ivory gold male, bred by the authors.

will be inspected by a number of experienced judges who will recognize the birds with the finest qualities. Of course, birds receiving high honors in such shows must have priority in further breeding.

The art of canary breeding relies to a high degree on the manner of selection. In fact, the selection of parents able to produce near-perfect young can be described almost as an art form in itself.

Selection must consider *all* characteristics of each individual—the good with the bad, the desirable with the rejects. One cannot be too rigorous in selection!

Thus, the clever breeder selects his or her breeding stock well before

Breeding cages in a bird room.

the breeding season, choosing the combinations with the utmost care, often seasoned with a little intuition. In most cases, the breeder will select a second group of breeding birds, to use in case of emergency. This is much better than having to "panic buy" new stock after the season has begun.

Blood or Red Mites (*Dermanyssus*)

Occasionally, a hen may neglect to feed her young properly, or even abandon them altogether; the young may be weak and listless, or have a pale interior to the beak instead of a healthy red one.

One common cause of such anomalies is the blood mite, that is, large numbers of them. These unpleasant, minute parasites live in cracks and crevices in cages, aviaries, and bird rooms during the day, coming into the nests at night to suck the blood of nestlings and mothers, but disappearing again into their shelters before first light. Large numbers of them can severely weaken stock and are a threat to the success of the whole breeding season itself. If you suspect an infestation of mites, you must thoroughly clean and treat all areas in which they can operate. Use a commercial insecticide specially formulated to use in the proximity of birds. As prevention is always better than having to find a cure, make sure that nooks and crannies in cages and aviaries are kept to a minimum. Cracks, holes, and such can be easily filled with one of the excellent filler materials available on the market. The area is then sanded down and painted to leave a smooth, mite-free area (see also External Parasites, page 96).

Chapter Five

Understanding the Canary

A Little History

The class *Aves* includes all of the 9,500 or so species of modern birds, ranging in size from the huge flightless ostrich to the tiny hummingbird. In between, there are all shapes, sizes, and colors imaginable. It might therefore be considered remarkable that such a relatively insignificant little bird as the canary has in the past few hundred years developed to the point where absolutely everybody is familiar with it; it is, in fact, the world's most popular pet bird.

A person with barely any knowledge of biology will be able to recognize and identify the canary, though its scientific name (*Serinus canaria* or *Fringilla canaria*) is less familiar. Over the years, this little bird has changed dramatically from its relatively drab, wild ancestor and is now available in a rich variety of shapes and colors that the early canary breeders scarcely could have imagined. Related wild subspecies of canaries still can be found throughout Europe and parts of Asia, and

ornithologists—professional bird scientists—have divided canaries into various groups. The most important canary to the aviculturist, of course, is the one from the Canary Islands or Madeira, islands off the west coast of North Africa in the Atlantic Ocean. The color of this wild bird is mainly olive green, broken with a number of grayish brown (hen) or yellowish (cock) stripes. The yellow in the males is not very obvious and certainly no basis for comparison with current yellow canaries. No matter how drab and insignificant-looking the wild canary may be, it has the honor of being the ancestor of all current song, color, or type canaries!

Early Domestication

The early history of domestication is obscure, but there are a few fairly believable stories, one about the Frenchman, Jean de Bethancourt, who married a girl native to the Canary Islands. He settled on the islands and lived mainly from farming and fishing. He became fascinated by the songs of the wild canaries and started to build small

*A Corona Harz (right)
and a variegated canary.*

The Elba Canaries

Perhaps the best-known story is that of the Spanish ship that was caught in a storm off the coast of Italy as it proceeded to Livorno. The cargo consisted largely of canaries the sailors undoubtedly felt sorry for and, in their compassion, they released the birds. Thereafter, canaries were found on the island of Elba for some considerable period. From Elba, some found their way to the mainland; however, canaries are no longer to be found on Elba. The wild canary should not be confused with the European canary, which, ornithologically, is a totally different species. The European canary still can be found in Elba, but not the wild canary.

Harz Canaries

The original Elba refugee birds found the climate to their liking and multiplied. The Italians realized the momentary prospects of these sprightly little songsters, caught them in the thousands, and brought them to the mainland. The canaries made their way from there via northern Italy to the Tirol and to parts of Germany, where they were successfully bred and marketed. It was not long before they were found in England and Russia. It would seem that the prices of canaries were not too high, since most of them were kept and bred by the working classes. The poor mountain folk of the Harz

cages in his spare time. He began to fill these with canaries and ship them to Spain in Spanish vessels; thus, Spain would have been the pioneer country in caged canaries. This story must be accepted for what it is worth, though it really does not matter whether it is believed. It is certain, however, that during the sixteenth and seventeenth centuries, canaries already were being bred in several places. They are also alleged to have been bred in large numbers in Spain during the fifteenth century.

Another story tells of how Spain held a very tight rein on the canary market, exporting just a few males to Italy and Switzerland. A mistake seems to have been made, however, in one of these exports and a female got into the hands of a priest who started breeding her. It may be that this female was mistaken for a male due to her bright coloring or perhaps her song was like that of a male. Judgment on the authenticity of this story will again have to be reserved.

area in Germany bred the birds both for pleasure and profit. This is not to say that the Harz canary peddlers charged low prices. In this regard a colleague, C. Stork, wrote a letter to us that said:

"In our Low Countries (Holland) canaries were imported from Germany and Belgium particularly in the nineteenth and in the beginning of the twentieth centuries. The Netherlands already had some canary breeders herself, but apparently there was such a demand for canaries that the foreign peddlers had no trouble selling their birds. These peddlers were a common sight in our towns and villages at that time. They carried on their backs a wooden rack which had a great many little cages attached to it, with four to six canaries in each cage. The whole contraption was tied to the back of the peddler with belts and was covered with a canvas, which was rolled up in good weather. The peddler could be heard coming from quite a distance, because the birds had grown accustomed to their nomadic existence and sang to their heart's content.

"These peddlers traveled from town to town and from village to village. They usually spent a few days in a particular lodging, awaiting buyers who were made aware of the peddler's visit by an advertisement placed in the local paper. With sales the cages became emptier, in contrast to the peddler's wallet; in the meantime, his supply of the niger seed with which he fed his canaries

was also steadily being depleted. The peddlers usually bred their own birds. They lived in the Harz, the Black Forest, in Zwaben, and in Bavaria, as well as in the vicinity of Liege. As soon as the breeding season was over and the young birds had started to sing, the peddler buckled his rack to his back and started the peddling journey. This was quite an achievement, especially when we consider that these travelings often lasted until the spring and that the peddler walked the entire way. Many of them often went back to the same lodgings, and they were generally considered the most honest because one could then feel assured that the peddler could be located if something ailed the purchased bird. These peddlers acquired a fair use of the Dutch language, and they must have made a very decent living, because good singers could procure as much as twenty guilders and more, and that in a time when a working man seldom earned more than ten guilders a week!"

Harz canaries also were found in England, a country that always had an important standing in avicultural matters. Soon England developed its own methods of operation with regard to canary development, and performed a splendid job in producing song canaries within its borders. Of course, the wild canaries' singing talents had to be further improved by selective breeding, the simplicity of which should not be underestimated.

In France, attempts were made to enrich the song of the canary with musical instruments. Hervieux de Chanteloup, who was connected with the court of King Louis XIV, described special little flutes made to accompany the canaries. He even tried to teach the canary to imitate the human voice, though unsuccessfully.

Hybrids

In 1750 the Dutch author F. Van Wickede wrote about color varieties that are well known and loved today. These include the agate (diluted green) and the isabel (cinnamon), the feuille morte, the white, and the yellow; even an albino seems to have existed, but not today. F. Van Wickede's writings about hybrids are also fascinating. In his time, the currently well-known crossbreedings with goldfinch, greenfinch, siskin, chaffince, and redpoll already were common. In fact, even crossings with the hedgesparrow and the wagtail were common! (We ornithologists find the possibility of such crossings difficult to believe.)

Singing Competitions

Quite a lot has happened to the wild canary since it was first brought into captivity. The color, the shape, and especially the song, have undergone considerable development. Originally, the nightingale was classed as the champion singer; the European goldfinch was a good imitator of other bird songs, but now the canary came into its own. The Germans were the pioneers and masters of the development of the canary's song. It is very interesting to attend a singing competition or an exhibition where song canaries are being judged. You will be astounded by the repertoire of "rolls" and "tours." These include the bass roll, the hollow roll, the water glucke, the schockel, and the hollow bell. The Harz roller canary or domestic Harz was developed for its song, and it is still much loved and bred today.

Type canaries also started to gain attention, each variety more or less having its own beginning followed often by an interesting history. These birds capture quite a share of the canary interest and should by no means be regarded as unsuccessful by-products of canary breeding.

The Canary and Literature

The canary has been domesticated for only about five centuries, starting at about the time printing itself was invented. So the canary has developed along with the printed word and some interesting and sometimes incredible details have been recorded. By reading these old texts, one realizes that even the breeders of long ago had a surprisingly good knowledge and background with regard to their care and breeding of birds.

The very first mention of the canary in literature probably occurred in the year 1555, when the Swiss naturalist Konrad von Gesner described it in his *Avium Naturae* (*Natural History of Birds*). Although Gesner had never seen a canary, the details had been given to him by colleagues who had. Gesner called the canary *Canaria Avicula*. At that time the canary also was known as a cane or sugarcane bird, probably derived from the fact that there was a sugarcane industry on the Canary Islands. However, this also led to an erroneous belief, even to modern times, that sugar is good for canaries. The occasional treat with a little sugar certainly will do no harm, but habitual feeding with sugar can make a bird obese.

An Italian scholar, Aldrovandi, who was connected to the University of Bologna, wrote about the canary in one of his many papers and stated that the cock can be distinguished readily from the hen by his more intense yellow color; he also included an illustration. In 1622 a book by G. Olina was published in Rome; it contained a very beautiful illustration of a canary, which can be found repeatedly published in later works. Toward the end of the nineteenth century, the experts in the field included Dr. Karl Russ (Germany), Josiah Blagrove (England), and A. Nuyers and J. H. Beekman (the Netherlands). All four wrote informative and interesting material. Today, there is no shortage in the amount of literature available on canaries.

A book by R. van der Mark, *Kanaries houden als liefhebberij* (*Keeping Canaries as a Hobby*), illustrates the intensity of the efforts of breeders in the Harz Mountains and particularly in St Andreasberg. He writes:

"The village (of St. Andreasberg) has some 3,800 inhabitants with 800 families, of which 600 are occupied with canary breeding. The women, in particular, take care of the birds. The manufacture of song cages, transport cages, 'song cabinets,' and other necessary equipment for canary breeding is an important industry. In 1881 St. Andreasberg bred no less than 24,000 Harz canary cocks, which were exported all over the world for high prices, because the quality of these birds was world famous."

Decline in Canary Breeding

Canary breeding was, for many years, the chief industry in the Harz region, though this position has, for some time, been ousted by tourism. A decline in the industry already was apparent by 1885, when an increase of infertility and weakness caused chicks to die in the nest. Unfortunately, the quality of the song also declined. Skillful breeders who had not followed the regimented and continuous pattern of breeding still received high prices for their birds—about 75–100 Deutsche marks, a considerable amount for that time. However, the "in-breeders" ran into problems, with exports to England, Russia, and the United States showing a dramatic decline. They endeavored to avoid competition by resorting to the old trick of selling males only, with the tragic consequence of countless females being destroyed. However, this was a matter of honor among the mountain inhabitants, as it was a means of confining breeding to particular villages. During World War I, some of the inhabitants of St. Andreasberg traveled to the Dutch border where they exchanged cock and hen canaries for groceries, especially coffee. The heyday of St. Andreasberg and the entire Harz region is over, but the name of the Harz canary will ever remind fanciers of the geographical origin of many great canary breeding achievements.

Canary breeders in Belgium gained excellent reputations for their world-famous waterslagers, later adding various type varieties to their achievements. Fanciers in The Netherlands also have not been idle, and thousands of quality color and type canaries of Dutch origin find their way annually to all parts of the globe. The Belgians and Dutch have a reputation for very high standards at their canary exhibitions. Their countries often attain the highest

honors and first prizes in international competitions. When Mendel's Law became common knowledge, this breeding was perfected.

The Canary— Inside and Out

What does a canary look like from the inside? A diagram can show the skeleton of a bird—the structure of its bones, the framework that holds the bird together. As with most birds, the skeleton of the canary is extremely light and finely built, a necessity to enable the bird to fly.

Bones

Although the bones are thin, they are amazingly strong, as they contain more calcium than the bones of mammals. Just imagine the amount of work and shock the apparently fragile little feet of the canary must experience, as the bird springs from one perch to the next.

To make the bones even lighter, they contain a honeycomb of air pockets (pneumatized; filled with air). These reduce the weight without decreasing the strength of the bone;

Canary bones are very light and prone to fracture; many are not much thicker than eggshells and are hollow. These pneumatized bones (cross section), with struts and air sacs or medullary cavities, act like air reservoirs (most of the large bones have air sacs which penetrate down deeply into the bones). The keel-shaped breastbone presents excellent room for attachment of the powerful flight muscles.

compare this with a hollow bicycle frame. The skull and the upper neck vertebra are connected by an extremely efficient joint, which enables the bird to turn its head 180 degrees, very important if the bird is to be able to preen most of its feathers. Moreover, it enables the bird to tuck its head between the feathers when sleeping.

The upper mandible sits immovably on the skull; the lower mandible is connected to the skull at the quadrate and can move independently. Canary breeders are required to know this fact; when they administer medicine or feed young birds, it is the *lower* mandible that must be pulled down, in order to open up the mouth.

The hardest part of the canary's beak is at the tip and around the edges. This is necessary, as the bird must be able to dehusk hard seeds. The remaining parts of the beak are softer. The beak is covered with a fine membrane, which if injured, could lead to infection.

The strongest and heaviest bones of the canary are those in the breast and in the wings. These are more important to a flying bird that those of the legs and feet, which can be less strong. With flightless birds, such as the ostrich, a paradoxical situation exists in which the leg bones are stronger than those of the breast and wings.

Skeleton of a canary:
1. Skull
2. Foramen
3. Upper mandible
4. Lower mandible
5. Vertebrae column
6. Clavicle
7. Coracoid
8. Sternum
9. Patella
10. Phalanges
11. Tarsus
12. Tibia and fibula
13. Femur
14. Pelvis
15. Pygostyle
16. Ischium
17. Ribs
18. Scapula
19. Hemerus
20. Radius
21. Ulna
22. Carpals
23. Metacarpus
24. Phalanges

Birds have many pneumatized bones, or bones filled with air. Most of the large bird bones have air sacs that penetrate down deeply into these bones; however, these air passages may be a real problem in cage and aviary birds as there are internal parasites living within the respiratory system. One of these mites is the air sac mite (*Sternostoma trachaecolum*), which has a serious effect on the health of various bird species such as canaries, Gouldians, and many other fancy finches. Most airborne treatments simply drive the air sac mite deeper into the air sacs, where it patiently waits for the gas to pass. Systemic (in the blood) treatments are therefore more effective at controlling these mites than are airborne treatments, in any case, consult a knowledgeable avian veterinarian (see also page 97).

Wings

In order to use the wings, the bird must have highly developed muscles. The flight muscles are attached to the wide and flat sternum (breastbone). The sternum is attached to the vertebral column (backbone) via the ribs, and via the coracoid to the furcula (wishbone). The limbs are affixed to the pelvic girdle at the joint known as the acetabulum. In the canary, the femur (thighbone) and the upper parts of the fibula/tibia are inside the abdomen.

The wing skeleton of a bird consists of the humerus (upper arm bone), the ulna and radius, and the manus, which is attached to the ulna and radius by the ulnare and radiale and consists of the carpometacarpus and digits 1–3. In canaries and many other birds, there is a special tendon that prevents the bird from falling off its perch when it sleeps. This works as follows: The muscles that clench the toes end in a tendon that passes along the outer edge of the joints. When the toes are clenched over a perch, and the bird relaxes downward, the tendon locks the toe muscles into place and the bird remains fixed until it straightens its joints up again.

Internal Organs

Stomach: A look at the internal organs reveals that the stomach is situated in the middle of the body. It is divided into two "compartments," the priventriculus and the ventriculus or gizzard. The stomach of a seed-eater is a very important organ as the bird cannot chew the seeds it eats; the stomach thus must grind up the food as an aid to digestion. Digestion in most birds also is assisted by a crop, which is a sort of storage bag for food, where the beginnings of digestion take place. The food slowly passes from the crop into the proventriculus, where stronger digestive juices are poured upon it before it passes to the gizzard; a bird's digestive juices are generally stronger than those of mammals.

Gizzard: The gizzard has extremely muscular walls and is lined with a tough, leathery membrane. The whole organ is designed to grind up food, such as hard seeds, into a digestible pulp. Small stones and pieces of grit that the bird has swallowed sit in the gizzard and assist with the grinding. These stones and

Some internal organs of the canary:

1. Lungs	**9. Caecum**
2. Esophagus	**10. Anus or vent**
3. Crop	**11. Duodenum**
4. Proventriculus	**12. Pancreas**
5. Gall	**13. Spleen**
6. Jejunum	**14. Kidneys**
7. Illeum	**15. Liver**
8. Small intestine	**16. Ventriculus**
	or gizzard

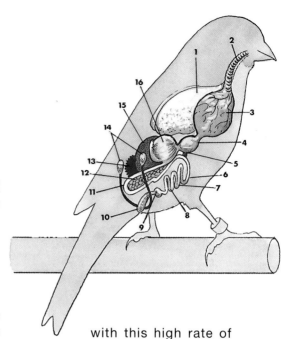

grit eventually are worn away and pass on through the system, which is one of the reasons why it is important to keep your canaries with a constant supply of grit; the other reason, of course, is that part of the grit itself provides the body with essential minerals.

Intestines: From the gizzard, the ground-up food passes into the intestines, which in a canary are relatively long due to the type of food it eats. In a bird of prey, for example, that feeds on meat that is relatively easier to digest, the intestines are much shorter.

Cloaca: The intestinal canal ends at the cloaca, a sort of general purpose sac, into which the ureters also pass, as well as the oviducts in the hen and the seminal duct of the cock.

Metabolism: All birds have a relatively fast metabolism, which is connected with the relatively high body temperature and energy requirement. Small aviary birds, including the canary, have a normal body temperature of 106 to 107°F (41–42°C), a positive "fever" when compared with most mammals!

The food requirement of birds therefore has a strong connection with this high rate of metabolism. Birds, including canaries, cannot survive for long without food. As seeds are relatively poor in nutrients, the canary also must eat a lot of them before it gets its full quota. Depending on the season, these little birds will eat 10 to 20 percent of their own body weight every day! The food requirement of the birds (proteins in particular), especially the hens in the breeding season, increases dramatically.

Air sacs: As well as in the bones, small air sacs are found in other parts of the canary's body. These also help to keep the overall weight of the bird down and, additionally, act as a supplementary store of oxygen. During flight, the bird requires extra amounts of oxygen, which it gets from the large lungs *and* the connected air sacs.

The Outside of a Canary

What about the outside of a canary? There are many interesting and important facts to learn about the various "parts." The feathers are particularly important to both the fancier and the canary. Indeed, if canaries did not have feathers there would be surely very few canary fanciers. The fancier is interested in the colors and condition of the feathers, but to the birds, the feathers have three major functions:

• They insulate against extremes of temperature.

• They provide the possibility to fly.

• They form a secondary sexual characteristic.

The first of these functions is very clear. By trapping pockets of air between the feathers, good insulation is achieved. In cold weather the feathers are fluffed out, trapping more air, which is a bad conductor of heat, whereas in warmer weather, the air is expelled so that some heat can be lost. A canary therefore looks "fatter" in cold weather than in warm. Birds that require an even greater insulation against the cold for reasons of habitat (ducks, for example) have a relatively larger number of feathers.

Feathers are situated in certain areas of the skin. There are thickly feathered areas and almost bald areas. The feathers themselves, however, protect all parts of the body surface. During the annual molt, the old, worn-out feathers are shed and replaced by new ones. In the canary, the molt begins on the shoulders and the tail, then the neck, breast, belly, and wings in turn. Therefore, not all feathers are shed at once, making the bird bald, and it can continue to fly as the primary and secondary flight feathers gradually are renewed.

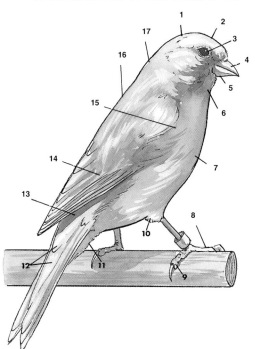

Knowing these different parts of a canary's exterior is especially useful when dealing with breeders, judges, and avian veterinarians.

1. Crown	*8. Front toes*
2. Forehead	*9. Back toe*
3. Eye	*10. Tibia*
4. Upper mandible or upper beak	*11. Cloaca and undertail coverts*
5. Lower mandible or lower beak	*12. Tail and upper-tail coverts*
6. Chin, malar region, and throat	*13. Rump*
	14. Wing
	15. Bend of wing and shoulder
7. Jugulum and breast	*16. Back*
	17. Nape

Tame Canaries

Canaries are naturally active and intelligent. It takes little time for them to discover which member(s) of the household are mostly involved in their care and management. Fanciers with garden aviaries, for example, know that the birds will wait by the aviary wire when fresh food is being brought in the mornings. Canaries generally are not fearful or shy and soon adapt to most situations. Those who care for them are regarded as friends. However, this does not mean that a canary becomes as tame and trusting as a parrot or parakeet. One exception is a canary that has been hand-reared, one that has been lovingly and carefully raised to independence. It will regard the person who hand-reared it as one of its own kind, not as a human being, but as another canary. A cock bird will sing and court his attendant, whereas a hen will offer an invitation to mate! In all probability, the bird sees mainly the head and face of its attendant, especially the eyes and mouth, but also the hands that provided the food and played an important role in the development of the chick.

To gain good eye contact with a tame, hand-reared canary, you can encourage it to sit on the palm of your hand or on your finger and hold it about 12 inches (30 cm) in front of your face. The shoulder is another favorite spot; the bird has a firm perch from which it can look around without fear of falling, and eye contact is easy to maintain. It won't be long before the shoulder is a favorite landing spot for your free-flying, tame canary.

There are, of course, canaries that will steadfastly refuse to get so tame that they will sit on the hand or shoulder. Such behavior often arises from a bad experience that may have occurred with catching and gripping. A good indication that a tame canary is not particularly afraid of the finger or hand is when it will sing or attempt to mate with the offered hand.

If the understanding between attendant and bird is not deep, then the canary will substitute an article from the cage or the room as its "steady partner," for example, a yellow ball or other toy—even a plastic bird—or its own reflection in a mirror. Do not be anxious if you observe such behavior in your tame, hand-reared canary; it is behaving naturally.

Such a tame canary really cannot be compared with, for example, a tame cockatiel or parakeet, but with gentle and loving care, it is possible to get a canary quite tame.

In general, however, the canary fancier is less concerned with this aspect of the hobby than with breeding, color, and song points.

Chapter Six

Disease Prevention and Cure

Signs of Illness

Once you have acquired healthy canaries, it is your job to keep them that way and to prevent any diseases. Your whole hobby is dependent on the health of your stock, not just on breeding successes or failures. If you start with unhealthy or inferior stock, then you must expect runs of bad luck and disappointment; this is why many

A sick canary, with swollen or dull eyes and puffed-up feathers, often looks like a pitiful ball of feathers hiding in a corner or under a food dish, sleeping with its head burried deeply in the feathers.

beginners have given up shortly after starting.

Sickness in a canary breeding establishment is a disaster both in direct and indirect ways. Sometimes a sick bird apparently gets better, but is still carrying the disease organisms. Such an event certainly can lead to inferior breeding results and the possibility of the disease being carried over to the offspring.

Sickness must, therefore, be prevented at all cost. Good accommodations and daily care for the birds' welfare will go a long way toward this end. Your birds will not, or rarely, suffer from disease and will remain in top condition. You then can expect good results from them, and you will not be disappointed.

Even with the best of care, some canaries may fall ill, especially when all the circumstances are not known. But canary breeders who know their stuff and inspect their birds daily and diligently will be able to nip potential disasters in the bud, long before those who don't. Immediate action can then be taken before it is too late.

A healthy canary is a nimble, cheerful bird with tight plumage, bright, open eyes, a hearty voice, and the droppings should appear normal. There are no mites on it, it sings with the joy of life, it stands high and proudly on its feet, and is a picture of activity.

The sick canary is exactly the opposite. It sits on its perch with its feathers ruffled out. If it eats at all, it only picks at its food. It does not fly or sing. It allows itself to be trifled with, and lets its smart coat hang sorrowfully. It sleeps too much and sits on two feet instead of just one as a healthy bird does.

By now, the negligent fancier must have realized that something is wrong, but it is probably already too late. The more diligent fancier, however, perhaps will have detected a certain hoarseness in the bird's voice well before the more serious symptoms arose. He or she may have seen the bird sleeping at a time when it usually is *not* sleeping and will know this as a warning that something is amiss and will have to keep an even closer eye on the bird.

Inspect the droppings at all times. The normal dropping has three components:

1. *Feces*: solid and tubular in shape; the color ranges from light to dark green (almost black)

2. *Urates*: pasty, light cream to white in color; irregularly wrapped on or around the feces

3. *Urine*: clear, odorless liquid portion of the dropping

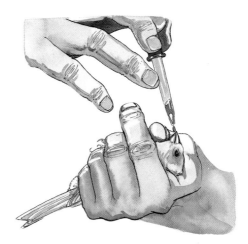

Sometimes a plastic eyedropper is essential in the administration of vitamins or medicine according to your veterinarian's specifications.

A color change, or thin and watery droppings, is a sure indication that the bird is ailing.

The First Actions to Take

One may think that the first action to take is to find out exactly from what disease the bird is suffering, but this is not the case. The most important thing to do first is to catch the bird *immediately* and place it in a warm place or, preferably, in a hospital cage. A hospital cage (see page 89) should be part of the standard equipment for all canary breeders. The bird will find peace and warmth in the cage, factors it requires for its cure. The bird must be given food and water, placed within easy reach, and studied more carefully.

The symptoms will give some clues to the nature of the disease and experienced fanciers may know, with some degree of accuracy, what is wrong; however, the diagnosis of many bird diseases is not easy. Even the veterinarian sometimes has great difficulty in recognizing bird diseases. The specialized bird veterinarian may find the cause after extensive examination of the bird.

Beginners therefore must not risk further treating the bird until they have obtained expert advice as soon as possible. Fortunately, most diseases are easily diagnosable from the symptoms, even for beginners and, fortunately, most of them can be treated with just the application of warmth and rest.

A qualified avian veterinarian is the best person to treat a sick bird, but it makes sense for fanciers to learn as much as they can about diagnosing and treating bird diseases. However, *extreme caution* must be taken in the administration of any medicines; ask the doctor for guidelines.

Closer Inspection

The fancier will always try to save the life of a sick bird, even a "cheap" bird deserves to live. After a few hours in the hospital cage, a closer inspection of the sick bird can be made.

1. Blow the feathers around the vent apart and see if the area looks dirty and/or slimy. If this is the case, it will indicate some kind of digestive problem or enteric infection.

2. See if there are dark marks on the skin of the belly, which can mean a liver infection and it is best to consult a veterinarian without delay.

3. Feel the flesh on either side of the breastbone; if it feels limp, this is another indication that the bird's health is suffering.

4. Weeping or wet nostrils and wheezing can mean aspergillosis, a disease that is almost incurable and is caused by inhaling spores into the respiratory system, but fortunately in most cases it is a minor respiratory infection about which the veterinarian can do something.

5. More serious is when the bird has difficulty getting its breath. Panting with the beak open can mean canary pox. Look for the pustules on the toes, the base of the beak, and along the edges of the wings.

6. If the bird is newly sick and is continually scratching, it could be infested with mites. A hen bird could be suffering from egg binding. If, after the examination, you have not found any diagnostic symptoms, take another general look at the bird. Perhaps you will find a swelling or a broken wing or leg; perhaps the bird has an eye infection and shows inflamed areas around the eyes.

Try to think of any other cause. Is the diet in order? Is there a shortage of calcium, vitamins, or proteins? Was the drinking water polluted? Could the bird have hypothermia? Was the food "off?"

If you suspect that the bird is failing in anything, it is easy to take the appropriate action. If you cannot find what is ailing the bird, place it back in its warm hospital cage. *Do not give it any medicine unless you act on the advice of a veterinarian.*

Treatment

Hospital Cage

The first part of treatment is the application of warmth. A sick bird must be isolated in a warm place immediately after it is discovered. The isolation will, of course, help protect the other birds from the disease if it is infectious, and the warmth is the first part of the treatment. In winter, one naturally can bring the sick bird into a warm room in the house, but it is even better to put the bird in a place where the temperature can be maintained between 85 to 90°F (29–32°C). The best way of doing this is to use the hospital cage.

Hospital cages can be bought from avicultural suppliers, but even the mediocre handyperson can make one. It consists of a glass-fronted box cage about 16 × 16 × 16 inches (40 × 40 × 40 cm). Four 60-watt tungsten light globes should be installed in the roof of the cage so that each works independently. This will allow the correct temperature to be achieved in the cage, whatever the temperature is outside. The bulbs are separated from the main area of the cage by a sheet of nonflammable material. Sheet metal is probably best for this as it quickly will conduct the heat through the cage and it will protect the bird from the glaring light.

An easy-to-read thermometer should be affixed to one wall inside the cage. A sliding tray in the base of the cage can be covered with paper, which should be changed twice a day, as the droppings of a sick bird are likely to be infectious.

Note: In evaluating a sick bird it is important to monitor its excretion daily. This can be done only if the material on the cage bottom lends itself to that evaluation; therefore, in the morning and late afternoon use paper towels, newspaper, or something impervious to water that will allow for this evaluation.

A wire screen installed above the tray will allow the droppings to fall through and prevent the bird from getting soiled. Although the sliding glass front is movable, it is more convenient to have an additional small service door in one of the ends, so that food and water can be

An original hospital cage, available in the better pet shops, is designed to isolate and monitor sick birds. It provides warmth necessary for the recovery of many birds from a variety of illnesses.

given, water especially, because the warm bird is likely to get very thirsty.

Ventilation: Although the bird must be kept warm, it should not be denied adequate ventilation. In such a small, warm area, fresh air must be available, but without causing drafts. This can be achieved by drilling a few small holes near the top of the ends of the cage.

Cleaning: After each use, the hospital cage should be thoroughly scrubbed, disinfected, rinsed, and dried inside and out, ready for the next emergency.

Warning: Be sure to disconnect the electricity supply before wetting the cage!

Hygiene

When dealing with sick birds, strict hygienic measures are essential; therefore, give the birds good clean food and water, fresh green food and freshly prepared soft food. Clean up any mess and droppings as often as necessary and do not forget your own personal hygiene. You will not want to be the culprit spreading the disease from one of your birds to the next.

In many cases, the sick bird will be cured after a spell in the hospital cage and no other treatment. Warmth works wonders when it comes to sick birds.

Reexamination

If the bird does not get better, examine it carefully again. Look especially at the droppings; if these are thin and watery or milky, then an enteric disorder is very likely. A small

dose—1–2 drops every four hours—of Kaopectate or Pepto-Bismol, or a little (point of a knife) sodium bicarbonate (baking soda) in the drinking water works wonders with canaries suffering from such ailments. If you find an infestation of mites while examining the bird, you should dust between the feathers or spray with special insecticide, and clean and disinfect housing and its "equipment." There are several brands available for use with small birds.

Any wounds or sores, infected areas around the beak or eyes, should be treated with a small amount of antibiotic ointment, styptic powder, cornstarch, baking soda, or boric acid.

If, after your careful examination, you still cannot find the cause of your bird's sickness, you must take the bird to a veterinarian. An experienced avian veterinarian soon will diagnose the disease and be able to administer the appropriate treatment. There are many excellent medicines available today for all sorts of ailments, and whatever treatment the veterinarian advises should be administered explicitly according to his or her instructions; remember, an overdose often can be more fatal than the disease itself.

Diseases and Injuries

The following alphabetical list presents the better-known bird diseases and injuries, their prevention, and treatment. There are other rare diseases, though, that are not included. *If you are unsure of the cause of your canary's sickness, you should seek expert advice from an avian veterinarian or an experienced fancier.*

Aspergillosis

This is an unpleasant, often fatal fungal disease of the respiratory system, which can invade the lungs and air sacs. It is caused by the bird breathing in the spores of *Aspergillus fumigatus*, which is common in damp or moldy hay, straw, chaff, seeds, moldy bread ("green" mold), and so on. With advanced infection, the respiratory passages and air sacs become filled with a yellow, cheeselike pus that seriously interferes with the bird's breathing. The bird will lose its appetite and will, of course, become seriously weakened. Once it reaches this stage, it usually is fatal. So be sure to consult your veterinarian immediately if you suspect aspergillosis. Recent good results (over 70 percent success) have been achieved using ketoconazole. For lung and air sac aspergillosis, ketoconazole is often delivered through nebulization (aerosol therapy, which we don't like!) or by injection into a muscle, or directly into the blood stream, or into the trachea. Amphotericine-B might also be helpful.

Always give clean, dust-free, dry seeds, except for freshly prepared soaked seed or germinated seed that should not have been musty or moldy before use, to your birds. Do not keep seeds near stores of hay, straw, or similar items, especially if they have been allowed to get musty. Stables and other animal houses where hay and straw frequently are used often become a reservoir for aspergillosis growth, so it is really best to keep your bird aviaries well away from such places. If a case should occur in your stock, correct your management/husbandry immediately, which includes consistent cleanliness and proper nutrition. Finally, disinfect cages and aviaries with a 1 percent copper sulphate solution and allow to dry before returning the birds.

Balance Problems

Canaries occasionally become disoriented due to extremes of temperature. On very hot or very cold days, for example, some birds may experience problems in coordinating their movements, maintaining their balance, or even flying straight. Changes in blood pressure due to the temperature can bring about such problems. In most cases, the symptoms will disappear as the bird's body adjusts to the temperature.

More serious is an infection of the middle ear, which includes the organ of balance. A sick bird will hold its head on one side and will have difficulty in maintaining its balance on the perch as well as an inability to fly straight. Such a bird requires immediate hospitalization and antibiotic treatment as prescribed by an avian veterinarian.

Bald Spots

Loss of feathers in certain parts of the body can be caused by a number of things, including external parasites (see page 96 for treatment). Sudden temperature variations also can cause feather loss. Outside aviaries that are partially or even completely enclosed with glass can become literal heat traps on hot summer days, whereas the temperature may dramatically drop at night. Bald spots often appear on the head as a result of this variation. Greater care should be taken in your aviary design to counter this problem.

During the annual molt, bald patches are, of course, natural, though the birds should not lose too many feathers all at once.

Canary Pox

There are various pox diseases suffered by different groups of birds and all are caused by certain strains of a virus. A virus is an organism that is so minute it cannot be seen under a normal microscope, let alone the naked eye. To see a virus an electron microscope is required. However, there are medical means of detecting or confirming viral infections without actually having to see them. The canary pox virus is difficult to destroy and canaries are quite susceptible to attacks.

Symptoms: Visible symptoms include the typical skin pustules, which in canaries are about less that ⅛ inch (1–3 mm) in diameter and yellowish to brownish in color. The first point of appearance is usually on the eyelids, then the feet and legs, and finally the entire skin. In some cases, the canary gets better after being under the weather for a few days—just as in a case of human chicken pox—but more often the infection spreads into the mouth and respiratory organs and usually becomes fatal.

Transmission: It is recommended that an outbreak of canary pox disease be referred to an avian veterinarian. Most attacks in canaries occur in youngsters of four to seven months of age and the death rate can be as high as 100 percent. Again, prevention is better than cure—there really is none—the first line of action being hygiene to prevent the transmission of the disease. The infected bird can pass the virus to other birds through saliva, nasal mucus, tears, and particles of skin, especially from broken pustules.

Mosquitoes especially can transmit the virus. Wild birds such as sparrows and finches, which also are susceptible to closely related strains of the virus that could infect the canary, can carry the disease to your stock. You could even be the culprit by walking into an infected aviary and carrying contaminated particles on your shoes to the next aviary.

Immunization: Vaccination against the disease is possible and usually available through your veterinarian. It is recommended that all canary keepers with valuable stock should have their birds immunized. The vaccine is injected into the wing membrane from below. It contains a weakened strain of the virus that will multiply in the bird, though it will not be strong enough to make it really sick, but it will be enough to persuade the bird's own immune system to produce antibodies that will kill off the viruses and protect the bird against the disease for the rest of its life.

Action: In case of an outbreak, the following measures must be taken:

• Isolate each bird from the infected cage and have each vaccinated by the veterinarian. Additionally, 250 mg of tetracycline and 5,000 units of vitamin A should be given. There is a good chance that this treatment will prevent further infection and save the birds from certain death.

• The pox blisters in infected birds should be dabbed with 1 to 3 percent merbromin in 70 percent alcohol. (Use mercurochrome from Hynson, Westcott and Dunning Inc., Baltimore, Maryland.)

• Hygiene is paramount! A footbath should be placed at the aviary entrance. Take off shoes, put on rubber boots, and walk through disinfectant when entering and leaving the aviary or bird room. If possible, wear an overall and a hat inside the aviary and remove them when you go out, leaving them in the entrance porch for use next time.

• All parts of an infected aviary or bird room, plus utensils, must be disinfected thoroughly. Regularly use a new solution so that disinfecting power is not reduced. After dis-infecting, thoroughly rinse all surfaces with fresh water and allow to dry completely before reintroducing healthy birds (cleared by the veterinarian).

Two vaccines appeared on the market in 1990: Pacheco's vaccine and a new canary pox vaccine. The latter comes in a freeze-dried form along with a diluting agent in which to dissolve it just before use. For further information on this new canary pox vaccine, speak to your veterinarian or write to Biomune Co., 8906 Rosehill Road, Lenexa, Kansas 66215.

Constant Overeating

Birds will tend to overeat constantly if given too much of certain foods. Canary grass seed is one such culprit; sweet foods are others. The overeating habit often develops in the nest, when the young are given too much rearing food. Sweet foods and canary grass seed are deficient in some nutrients. Birds should be given only good brands of rearing food and the foods suggested in the chapter on feeding. Dirty aviaries, stress, boredom, and vitamin deficiencies are other causes of overeating, which can be a stubborn and debilitating condition.

A bird with an overeating problem will look unwell, sitting at the food dish most of the time, with its wings drooping. It may look thin and undernourished as it is most probably overeating the wrong kinds of food. The feces of an affected bird are usually grayish black. And the bird may succumb to a secondary infection.

The first action to take is to adjust the diet. Sweet food should be avoided and no universal food or self-prepared egg foods should be given for about 20 days. Since bored and/or food-satisfied canaries have the "nasty" habit of sitting in their food dish, smaller cups and closed feeders are therefore preferable for obvious reasons.

Constipation and Diarrhea

Constipation: Constipation is, fortunately, rather rare in canaries but it can be very distressing to the bird when it occurs. The sick bird will restlessly flap its tail up and down as it strains to have a bowel movement. Causes of constipation include too much egg food, a bad diet, or, particularly, an excess of grit intake (grit impaction). Via radiography, tumors may be revealed, or a "stuck" egg, poor muscle tone, and obesity. Consult an avian veterinarian as soon as possible. In the meantime, correct the menu. A piece of apple will help soften the stool.

Diarrhea: Diarrhea generally is more serious than constipation and can be caused by a number of things including bad food, too much green food, obesity, respiratory or intestinal infections, excessive heat, or an excess of protein in the diet.

A bird suffering from diarrhea often is hunched up with its feathers fluffed out and listless. A bird with a serious case will often sit in a corner on the floor with its head tucked under its wing, having evidently lost all interest in life. It may drink quite a lot, which is a good thing, as diarrhea causes dehydration, but it may not eat much, if at all. The droppings will be very loose and watery and sometimes an unusual color depending on the cause.

It is always best to refer such cases to an avian veterinarian if you can, but there are one or two home remedies you may want to try. First, move the sick bird to a hospital cage and maintain the temperature at about 90°F (32°C). Chamomile tea can have a very good effect, whereas boiled rice, oat flakes, or millet sprays may help harden the stools. A commercial preparation called Norit may be used; dissolve a tablet of Norit in a tablespoon of water and administer a few drops into the beak of the sick bird, using a feeding syringe or medicine dropper.

Other causes of diarrhea include poor environmental conditions, such as bad ventilation, cold drafts, or sudden temperature changes. In outdoor aviaries, excessively cold drinking water can be a problem in the winter and, in any case, one should make sure that the water does not freeze over. Poisoning also could be a cause and you should take great care to make sure your birds and their food are not exposed to dangerous insecticides, fungicides, herbicides, and so on. If you suspect that one or more of your birds has been poisoned, you should place it in a warm cage, give it fresh green food, and add a little bicarbonate of soda to the drinking water (about 1 gram per full glass of water). Pepto-Bismol, or other purgatives also may be used but be very careful not to overdose. Bicarbonate of soda should never be given for more that two consecutive days. Consult your avian veterinarian immediately.

E. coli infection

This infection is caused by a gram-negative bacterium (*Escherichia coli* or simply *E. coli*) and can pose serious problems in canaries as well as many other bird species. *E. coli* can also be carried by humans and other animals; however, don't let anyone tell you that *E. coli* are normal residents of a bird's digestive system. They are certainly not, and, if they spread to other internal organs, they can quickly be fatal.

Good hygiene is the best preventive measure. Wash your hands every time you deal with your birds, especially when moving them from one cage or aviary to the next. Prevent fecal contamination of foodstuffs and work areas, and clean cages and furnishings frequently and thoroughly.

E. coli infection can be treated by administering three or four drops of Kaopectate or Pepto-Bismol to the sick bird every four hours with a plastic medicine dropper. This treatment coats and smoothes the inflamed lining of the digestive tract. If rapid improvement is not observed within 24 hours, consult an avian veterinarian, who may prescribe alternative treatments.

Egg Binding

This is unfortunately a well-known condition of captive birds that may be brought about by one or more factors. If birds are kept in optimum condition, egg binding is almost totally preventable.

Egg binding means that a gravid hen is unable to lay her fully-developed egg, due to multifactorial causes:

1. oversized or malpositioned egg

2. decreased muscle tone

3. not in prime breeding condition

4. low blood calcium due to overbreeding

5. damaged or infected uterus

6. obesity

7. malnutrition

8. sudden temperature changes

9. hereditary factors, such as a small body with a narrow pelvic outlet.

Another form of egg binding occurs when the eggshell has not developed properly, caused by a shortage of calcium or a malfunction in the mechanism that deposits calcium on the shell. The soft-shelled egg will not slide easily through the oviduct and is likely to get stuck. The prevention, of course, is to make sure that your birds get a balanced diet.

To further reduce the incidences of egg binding, do not breed birds too early in the season (late March or early April is early enough) and do not use birds that are too young or too old, as these are likely candidates for egg binding.

Treatment: Most egg binding usually can be cured. Using a dropper, place a few drops of mineral oil in the cloaca before placing the bird in a warm (hospital) cage, holding the temperature at 90°F (32°C). The combination of the warmth and the lubrication in the cloaca should enable the bird to pass the egg. An avian veterinarian usually can cure the problem by giving calcium, multivitamin, and oxytocin injections (oxytocin is a hormone that stimulates the oviduct to contract), and other medicines to stimulate contractions and muscle power to expel the egg. An egg laid after treatment is best discarded.

Egg Pecking

Though obviously not an illness in itself, egg pecking is a serious defect. A lack of calcium may be the cause but it is more likely to be boredom that starts the habit. Make sure that your birds get their usual quota of calcium-containing food supplements, and if the egg pecking persists, you may consider those suggestion for a cure described in Feather Plucking, page 100.

External Parasites

Parasites are creatures that live in (internal parasites) or on (external parasites) the bodies of others in order to survive, usually to the detriment of the host. In the present case, the host is the canary and the external parasites are all types of bloodsucking and biting invertebrates that may infest it if you are not diligent enough.

Red bird mites: The most serious external parasites are probably various mite species, the best known of which is the straightforward red bird mite, *Dermanyssus gallinae*, which spends the day hidden in cracks and crevices in the aviary or cage, but comes out at night, climbs on the birds' bodies, and sucks blood through the skin. A single mite, which is smaller than a pinhead, does not take much blood of course, but infestations of thousands of these pests can be very debilitating to your birds, making them anemic, through loss of blood, and causing stress because of the irritation the mites cause. Nesting birds can be constantly and severely tormented by these mites. Another problem is that the mites can carry diseases, such as atoxoplasmosis, from one bird to the next.

Always keep an eye open for the start of a mite infestation by inspection the cage or aviary and utensils. A white cloth left overnight in a corner of a cage or aviary will be used as a hiding place by mites if they are present. Tiny red creatures are easier to see against the white background; then you will know whether action is necessary or not.

Red bird mites can go for long periods without a blood meal and are, at such times, more difficult to detect as they will be translucent in color until they have a chance to feed on blood again. At a temperature of 68°F (20°C), the mites can reproduce every five days and can withstand severe frosts in the winter. These and other mite species can be introduced into your aviary at any time by wild birds, such as pigeons, starlings, or sparrows, sitting on or above your aviary roof preening their feathers. Or they may be introduced with new stock, especially birds from overcrowded stock aviaries. Another kind of mite, the northern fowl mite (*Ornithonyssus sylviarium*), actually breeds on the host and is more difficult to eradicate than than the red mite.

Burrowing mites: Another troublemaker is the burrowing mite, *Knemidokoptes pilae*. This little pest causes what is known in the fancy as scaly face, a term that is especially used by parakeet and other hookbill fanciers. The mite attacks the skin around the eyes and beak, and also, in serious cases or in various finch species, the legs and toes. These little arachnoidal parasites burrow into the outer layers of the skin and scales of the beak area and legs respectively, where they lay their eggs. If untreated, the resulting rough, scaly growths will gradually increase, and severe deformities of the beak or legs will occur. The condition will spread among the birds if no remedial action is taken.

Benzyl benzonate, petroleum jelly, or glycerin can be applied to the crusty, honeycomblike scales. Mineral oil can also be used, but be very careful to apply it only to the affected area and don't drip any on the plumage: Use a cotton-tipped applicator. Serious cases should be referred to an avian veterinarian for specialized treatment.

Any scale scabs that come away should be removed and burned, if possible. Clean and disinfect all areas in cages and aviaries to reduce the possibilities of further infection. Though not a particularly dangerous infection, it is troublesome and ugly, so take great care to prevent it. It is particularly common in parakeets (budgerigars), but the disease is, fortunately, rather rare in canaries and other large finches.

Air sac mites: The air sac mite (*Sternostoma trachaecolum*), is a bloodsucking arthropod that frequently affects various finches, especially Gouldian finches and related grass finches form Australia, and to a lesser extent, canaries. The mites infest the trachea, lungs, and air sacs.

An infection can occur in a mild or acute form. The mild form shows no specific symptoms other than the usual—for many infections—puffing out of feathers, ceasing to sing, moping, and slowly losing body condition.

At a later stage, as the mites infect the lungs and air sacs, the bird will develop obvious breathing difficulties (dyspnea). It will make swallowing noises, will wipe its beak repeatedly on perches or twigs, and will attempt to remove the mites from its air passages by coughing and spluttering. As the infection develops, the bird's labored breathing will be accompanied.by wheezing and peeping sounds, intermingled with little sneezes. In acute cases, the bird can suffocate from a literal plug of mites in the air passages. A microscopic examination will reveal numerous, dark-colored mites in the nostrils, the trachea, and all respiratory organs. Young mites usually are found in the nostrils.

For a long time it was thought that the birds expired through loss of blood, but this is not true; death occurs as a result of exhaustion caused by extreme dyspnea due to the presence of numerous mites in the trachea. The presence of the mites in a live bird is difficult to ascertain. A tracheal swab is required, but this job is obviously best left to an avian veterinarian.

Young mites can be expelled from the beak and nostrils through coughing and sneezing and easily can affect other birds through the food, water, or even by direct inhalation. Mites or their eggs are never, or very seldom, found in the birds' droppings, so there is no diagnosis to be found from that angle. We must be able to differentiate between a mite infestation and other respiratory conditions, such a diptheria (usually in canaries, other finch species, and doves, but rarely in Gouldian finches and other Australian grass finches), trachea worms, aspergillosis, and colds.

Besides what we already stated, there are a few methods that can be tried as treatment. One of these is what we like to call the "shake and bake" method; this has saved many of our birds, canaries as well as Gouldians and other species, from an almost certain death. The patient is placed in a paper sandwich bag containing a sprinkling of one teaspoon of five percent carbaryl (Sevin) powder. Not being very happy in the bag, the bird will flutter its wings and produce an effective dusting. An exposure of just five to ten seconds is adequate. Release the bird immediately back into its cage, which should be placed in a well-ventilated area. Do not be anxious about the powder getting in the birds' eyes. As you probably know, birds possess the so-called "third eyelid" (nictitating membrane), which protects the eye from irritation and abrasion. A complete cure usually is accomplished after a few days.

A one-time method of treatment is with Ivermectine (Eqvalan). The diluted (2.0 mg/ml) Eqvalan is injected at a dosage of 0.01 cc per 30 grams of body weight. This dosage is given only as a guideline of what has been found to be relatively effective in small birds in previous careful administration by avian veterinarians. The Ivermectine treatment has been used very successfully. The entire bird population in your cages and aviaries must be treated at the same time and the premises cleaned. Again, rely on your avian veterinarian, who should be extremely familiar with this treatment, as Ivermectine can be easily overdosed and losses can be alarming if it is used carelessly.

Other mites: Other mite species that may attack canaries include nondisease, relatively harmless species that live on the skin and feathers; one species, *Syringophilus bipectioratus*, may be found on many species of wild and domestic birds as well as canaries. Though they feed only on skin and feather debris, their irritating actions could be a trigger for feather plucking. A more serious species is *Dermoglyphus elongatus*, which actually burrows into the feather follicle; numbers of them can cause serious damage and spoil the plumage as well as distress the bird.

Lice: Though usually not regarded to be as serious as mites, lice also can pose a problem. There are several species that can be introduced to your stock in a manner similar to mites.

Insecticides: There are several proprietary brands of insecticides specially made for use in cages and aviaries, and on the bird themselves. Many of these use pyrethrin as the active ingredient. This organic insecticide is made from the pyrethrum flower, a kind of chrysanthemum, and it is quite harmless to birds if used as instructed. It will destroy lice, fleas, mosquitos, and other insect pests as well as ticks and mites. It may be available in fluid and powder form, the former being useful for spraying surfaces and utensils, the latter for application to the birds. Pay special attention to nooks and crannies and dark corners in your birds' accommodations. When treating individual birds, apply the powder throughout the plumage, paying special attention to the area around the neck, the vent, and under the wings, taking care not to get it in the eyes or mouth. Then place the birds in a separate cage

until the aviary or cage has been thoroughly disinfected and dried out. It is best to repeat the treatment after about ten days, so that any recently hatched pests are eliminated (the eggs often are not susceptible to the insecticide).

Eye Infections

Canaries are subject to various eye infections, most of which can be avoided if the birds are kept in optimum conditions. Many eye infections result from complications of other diseases, such as various respiratory infections. A deficiency in vitamin A, or even exposure to aerosol sprays, also can cause problems to the eyes. The bird usually will close the infected eye, which will be watery and the edges will be inflamed (blepharitis).

Bacterial infections can start as a result of unhygienic conditions. By wiping its beak on a fecally contaminated perch, for example, it is easy for bacteria to gain access to the bird's eye. Recently imported birds that have traveled in overcrowded conditions are a notorious source of eye infections, which can spread quickly from one bird to the next. (Each year, thousands of canaries are imported into the United States from Europe, especially Belgium and the Netherlands.)

A bird with infected eyes should be placed in a hospital cage or at least a warm environment. Apply an antibiotic ophthalmic ointment twice a day (ophthalmic Neopolycin or Neosporin are suitable products).

Such treatment usually will bring about recovery in a few days.

Feather Plucking

Feather plucking may occur toward the end of a normal or abnormal molt. The irritation experienced at this time may cause the bird first to scratch and finally progress to feather plucking. An infestation of external parasites also can set off a bout of it. Unfortunately, it does appear to develop into a difficult-to-cure habit once it has started, especially in hens.

Some hens will take to feather plucking if they have inadequate nesting material in the breeding season. It usually can be cured rapidly by supplying the hen with suitable nesting facilities and plenty of nesting material. Many breeders supply excess material in bunches suspended from the cage or aviary wire, to give the birds plenty to occupy themselves.

Occasionally, a hen, anxious to start on her next brood, will start to pluck the feathers from the young still in the nest from her previous brood. In such a situation, separate the young from the parents with a wire or bar partition. The young continue to be fed by the parents through the wire, but are safe from the feather-plucking beak of (usually) the mother.

Young birds also start feather pecking on occasion, especially if overcrowded in a small space. Such youngsters are usually pre-first molt, but independent. A good diet and plenty of space usually will cure the habit.

Once started in an aviary, the feather plucking habit is difficult to eliminate. Usually, one bird starts it and the others follow suit. The good fancier who observes each of his birds carefully every day will be able to catch a culprit before too much damage is done. The feather plucker must, of course, be removed and kept isolated in a roomy cage, where it should receive a good balanced diet and be given some treats (sticks, bells), and hemp or sisal fibers to play with. Birds that are the "victims" of the feather pluckers will show bald patches on the lower part of their backs. In serious cases, the bald patches also can be pecked raw and sore. Unfortunately, this attracts the attention of more canaries who also will begin to attack the victim. It should be obvious that such victims also must be separated immediately from the main flock before it is too late. The bird often can be returned safely once it is again fully feathered. Feather pluckers among lizard canaries are, of course, disastrous as the plumage is what makes these birds!

Fractures

The most serious fractures, which usually are fatal, are those of the neck or spine, which can be caused by a panicking bird flying into a solid surface, such as glass, wire, or wood. To avoid this, keep birds in a calm environment and make sure that nothing happens to give them sudden shock. Children and pets are often the culprits and should be taught to approach the birds in a calm and sensible manner, without excessive screaming and shouting, weeping and wailing, and gnashing of teeth. Semaphore signal practice and gymnastics should be performed well out of sight and sound of the birds. In fact, it is wise not to allow children to approach the birds without adult supervision.

A fracture of the wing stands a good chance of healing it you treat it the right way, but the bird may never again be able to fly properly. This problem is easily recognized as the bird will be sitting pitifully in a corner, incapable of flying and with the broken wing hanging down. Such an injury can happen during the catching of birds, unless great care is taken.

Once you locate the site of the fracture by gently feeling the wing, a little mild antiseptic should be applied. Many brands have the advantage of activating various glands to help speed up the healing process. If the skin is not broken, try to bring the bones together and hold them in position with adhesive plaster. After about 15 days, the wing should be healed and the plaster removed by cutting very carefully with sharp scissors. While healing, the bird should be isolated in a clean, comfortable cage without perches and with its food and water dishes within easy reach on the cage floor. Keep the bird as calm as possible—rest is an important aid to healing. Extra vitamin D, calcium,

and cod-liver oil are highly recommended. Fruit and egg food all help the healing process.

Broken, drooping wings can be bandaged best with gauze. Cut a slit in the gauze, then put the folded wing through the slit. Wrap gauze around the body and secure it to a leg to keep it from slipping off. Setting a broken wing is a difficult task, and it is better to entrust it to an experienced veterinarian.

In complicated or compound fractures, where the skin is broken and the bone often exposed, treatment is very difficult. In such cases it is probably best to put the bird out of its misery as, even if the wound heals to some extent, the wing usually will be badly set and the bird unable to fly.

Leg fractures also can occur through catching. Sometimes if the claws are too long they get caught in the cage or aviary wire and the bird breaks its leg in its efforts to escape. First disinfect the area of the fracture, then wrap a stiff bandage around it or make a splint using the insulation from a small segment of electrical wire. Straighten out the leg by carefully pulling a piece of thread tied to the foot. If the lower part of the leg is fractured, it is best to use a piece of electrical wire insulation or a quill splint about ½ inch (1 cm) long clasped to the fracture. The splint is fastened with a small piece of plaster or wrapped with cotton or wool yarn. Make sure that the fastening is not too tight or the circulation will be impaired. A thigh fracture is treated in a similar manner. In all cases it is obviously best to consult an experienced avian veterinarian.

The injured bird should be isolated in a cage with a layer of soft material, such as a thick layer of sand on the floor. Perches should be removed and food and water placed in a readily accessible spot. Give food supplements, as described above, and the leg should heal in about three to four weeks. If the leg should turn blue, then black, it means that it has died off (through a too tight splint or a bad join) and it will have to be amputated. In successful operations, the splint can be removed after four weeks.

"Spontaneous fractures," that is those without any apparent cause, are due to a mineral deficiency and should not occur if the birds are receiving a balanced diet containing vitamin D, cuttlebone, calcium, and green food.

Gout

Gout is an accumulation of urates and uric acids in various parts of the body, especially in joint spaces. If housing is adequate, the birds will have plenty of flying space and they will get enough exercise to keep their muscles toned and their circulation and respiration stimulated. This, coupled with a balanced diet, should be enough to prevent gout. If gout should occur, heat treatment of 80 to 85°F (27–30°C) and pure seed with a little powdered charcoal mixed in and a few drops of syrup of buckthorn in rice water will help alle-

viate it. Extra vitamin A and egg food also may help. Supply flat, soft, and broad perches—we suggest padding them with lamb's wool—and avoid exposure to cold and stressors. For pain relief, get allopurinal (Zyloprim), to decrease uric acid synthesis and cause the urate deposits to shrink.

Loss of Voice

A loss of voice or general hoarseness can be caused by several things. An infection of the respiratory tract, such as the common cold, will, of course, cause congestion in the larynx and will have to be treated as prescribed for colds. Some birds tend to be a little overzealous with their singing, resulting in hoarseness due to inflammation of the voice box. In such cases, the bird should be kept in a fairly small cage; covering it with a cloth, making sure it is placed in a spot where it cannot hear any other singing birds. A little honey or glucose added to the drinking water will help soothe the inflammation. Occasionally, one comes across a case of chronic hoarseness, which is an inheritable condition. Unfortunately there seems to be little that can be done about this condition.

Molting

All birds change their feathers at intervals. The feathers have to suffer a great deal of wear and tear from weather and wind, preening, courting, mating, nesting, brooding, and so on. Imagine how it would be if an average human worker wore his clothes day and night, nonstop for a whole year; they definitely would need changing! Thus, canaries have a complete annual feather change, or molt, once a year, immediately after the breeding season; the young of that season lose some of the body feathers, but not tail and wing feathers. The molt period usually takes place from the middle of summer until the middle of fall, so that the birds can enter winter with a clean, new coat.

The molt is thus closely connected with the reproductive cycle and takes place shortly after the most intense period of wear and tear: the brooding and rearing of young. A molt is not a sickness but a normal phenomenon; however, problem molts can and do arise. A good, problem-free molt is dependent on the season, temperature, humidity, and diet. A molt is usually more intense after a warm spring and start of summer than it is during cold and wet months. Sometimes a bird is apparently so eager to molt it continually will fluff out and shake its feathers, sometimes even plucking some out with its beak and clearly deriving some relief from doing so. Normally, however, the molt is a restful time for birds and they will avoid unnecessary activity. During the molt a bird's temperature is a little higher than normal, but if the molt is unsatisfactory, the temperature may drop.

Diet: Increased susceptibility to bone fractures occur at this time, due to the resorption of calcium from the bone tissues. Consequently, a rich protein diet and adequate calcium are required at the time of molting to provide fuel for the new feathers, which, in themselves, are 88 percent protein. A bird receiving a poor protein diet will not only grow a poor new set of feathers, it may even eat them to supplement its diet.

Abnormal molts: Sometimes a bird may have what is know as an abnormal molt, for example, losing too many feathers at once and having difficulty replacing them, or losing feathers in the wrong season. Such cases usually are triggered by extreme environmental factors, such as excessively high or low temperatures, sudden temperature changes, shock (sometimes called a shock molt), disease, or fear—all of which cause stress and upset the normal metabolism of the bird. A malfunction of the thyroid gland is often a cause of abnormal molt. Your veterinarian will determine if a dietary supplement is needed.

Shock molts can be avoided by keeping your birds in calm, peaceful surroundings where they are not subjected to sudden uproars or unwelcome visits from dogs, cats, owls, weasels, and other such animals. We frequently have seen birds contract a shock molt after being removed at night to be treated for a totally different disease! Strangely, wing feathers rarely are lost in shock molt, usually just small body and tail feathers. Sometimes, tail feathers are shed as a result of being grabbed by a predator, the latter ending up with a mouthful (or handful) of tail feathers while the bird makes its escape.

Permanent molts: Another kind of molt is known as "permanent" molt. This usually is caused by a shortage of proteins in the diet and, in such cases, the normal molt also may be incomplete. The problem usually can be corrected by adjusting the diet and perhaps improving the conditions. Introduce a high-protein diet and, in the colder months, supplementary heating, in the form of ceramic lamps, for example, can be provided. The use of a broad-spectrum fluorescent lighting, such as Vita-Lite, has been proven to have a beneficial effect on the health and vitality of birds during the short, dim winter days. This kind of lighting offers the biological advantages of natural sunlight, something that other artificial lights do not have. Such a light can favorably influence the metabolism of the bird by aiding in the production of vitamins in the body and fixing calcium in the bone tissues.

Obesity

Lack of adequate exercise and/or a diet too high in fat and carbohydrates can lead to obesity in a bird. The process of becoming too fat is rather slow, so canary owners should keep a careful watch on their birds. Birds that receive too many high-fat seeds, such as rape, linseed, niger seed, or sesame seed, scraps of sweet cake, cookies, and candies are subject to obesity. A really obese bird can no longer fly and barely can stand on its feet. It usually will sit on the cage floor panting and straining at every effort to move. The fat deposits will discolor the skin a yellowy color, which can be seen if the feathers are blown aside. An obese bird will die much sooner than a normal bird and it will be useless for breeding purposes. If a bird looks as though it is gaining too much weight, corrective action must be taken. Make sure that it is getting plenty of exercise. A caged bird should be allowed to free fly in a room for an hour or so each day. Also, hang some sisal ropes and millet sprays in the cage so that the bird is encouraged to be more active.

As far as the diet goes, give plenty of fresh greens and stick to the normal seed and pellet mixture with no high-protein or fatty foods.

Ornithosis

This is a disease also known as psittacosis, as it once was thought to be exclusive to parrots and parakeets. It is, however, found in many other bird species, even occasionally in canaries. It is a serious disease caused by *Chlamydia*, an obligate, intracellular organism. The disease occurs especially in birds housed and bred in unhygienic conditions and will spread quickly in overcrowded cages or aviaries. It often is brought in with imported birds, especially those that have been smuggled in.

Ornithosis can have a variety of symptoms and often is difficult to diagnose, especially in its early stages. It usually starts with a heavy

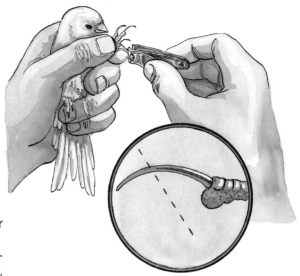

Clipping overgrown nails is easy. Be careful, however, not to cut the part of the nail that is supplied with blood (the "quick"), but if it does start to bleed, a moistened styptic pencil should be applied.

cold with the bird gasping and wheezing, often accompanied by a runny nose. Diarrhea and lethargy are further symptoms, and often, cramps and lameness appear just before death.

There is a milder form of the disease that sometimes can be cured. Unfortunately, however, the apparently cured bird remains infective to other birds and humans as a carrier throughout its life. The disease is classified as a serious hazard and is notifiable to the health authorities in several states.

In humans, the disease can be highly dangerous but the advent of certain antibiotics, especially the tetracyclines, have alleviated the danger to a great extent, always provided, of course, that you get timely diagnosis and treatment.

Overgrown Nails

Often referred to as "sickle" nails, this problem develops if the bird's nails do not get sufficient wear. If perches are too thin, for example, the ever-growing nails will not be touching the surfaces and, if untreated, even can grow into a long spiral. The answer is to provide perches of varying thicknesses, so that all parts of the toes and nails are continually

coming into contact with a surface as the bird moves from one location to the next. Overgrown nails can be dangerous, as they can catch in wire and possibly cause the struggling bird to break a limb. After fitting a suitable variety of perches, the overgrown nails must be trimmed back to a manageable length using a sharp pair of nail scissors or clippers

Hold the bird in the palm of the left hand (if you are right-handed) restraining it with three fingers, while you use the thumb and forefinger to manipulate one toe at a time. Hold the toe so that the light shines through the nail, and clip just below the quick (blood vessel). If you clip into the quick accidentally, you must stop the bleeding with a styptic preparation, such as kwik stop, though if you are careful, this will not be necessary. The clipped edge can be filed gently to a new point with a nail file.

Preen Gland Infection

The preen gland is normally the only skin gland possessed by birds. It is situated dorsally, just in front of the tail base, and secretes an oily feather conditioner, which the bird uses to condition and help waterproof its feathers. A little of the secreted oil is taken on the beak and wiped along the feathers during the process known as preening. This preen gland occasionally becomes infected and, such cases, a marked swelling will be apparent at the site of the gland. In apparent pain, the bird will peck and scratch at the offending spot and even may pull out some of the surrounding feathers. After a time, the abscess may burst, leaving signs of blood on perches. The alert fancier will not let the condition get this far, and will consult an avian veterinarian. A chronic infection usually arises from overproduction of preening secretion, so the condition can be relieved to some extent by gently squeezing out the gland at regular intervals. If this does not help, the avian veterinarian may have to operate. An incision with a scalpel at the appropriate spot will release the pus, and the infection can be syringed out and treated with antibiotics. Occasionally, the problem arises from a benign tumor of the preen gland. This also can be removed by the veterinarian, usually without complications.

Respiratory Infections

There is a range of infections of the respiratory tract, the most common of which are colds, causing inflammation of the nose and throat passages. These often occur in birds accommodated in cold, damp, and/or overcrowded conditions with poor ventilation. The organisms responsible for respiratory infections usually are present in the air in varying amounts. Normal, healthy birds usually have sufficient resistance against an invasion of these disease organisms, but unhealthy conditions cause stress and the resulting reduction in resistance. In severe cases, a simple cold soon can develop into fatal pneumonia if no action is taken.

As soon as cold symptoms arise in a bird it should be isolated in a warm place, preferably a hospital cage. Wipe away any nasal discharge with a cotton swab or similar item. Use a vaporizer to spray a fine, warm mist of water into the cage to soothe and moisten the inflamed respiratory tract. In all cases, an avian veterinarian should be consulted; remember that aspergillosis, ornithosis, and other unpleasant diseases often start with the symptoms of a cold.

Salmonellosis

There are hundreds of different bacteria species in the *Salmonella* genus, several of which can cause severe food poisoning in humans. In canaries and other birds, the rodlike salmonella bacteria are responsible for diarrhea, painful joints, and nervous disorders. The disease is transmitted by the feces and saliva of infected birds—accidental or intentional ingestion of feces or direct introduction to the young via the saliva of infected parents during feeding.

The disease comes in four forms, which can occur in any combination.

Intestinal form: The bacteria colonize the intestinal walls and interfere with digestion, causing foul-smelling, soupy, green, or brown slimy diarrhea, containing particles of undigested food. A green color in the droppings also can indicate a gallbladder infection—consult a veterinarian immediately!

Joint form: Once established in the intestines, the disease will break into the bloodstream and affect other parts of the body. In the bone joints, intense pain and swelling will occur and the infected bird will find difficulty in moving.

Organ form: In the bloodstream, the organisms can attack all internal organs such as the liver, kidneys, pancreas, heart, and various glands, causing severe malfunction of the metabolism and eventual death.

Nervous form: Salmonella affects the spinal column and nervous system, causing crippling, loss of balance, and paralysis. Typical symptoms include awkward turning of the neck, fouling of the vent region, and cramplike contractions of the toes.

Young birds infected in the nest usually die. Older birds may incubate the disease over long periods and become immune themselves, but remain carriers capable of transmitting it to other birds through their droppings or saliva. Hens are capable of transovarian infection.

Outbreaks of salmonelosis should be treated by a veterinarian.

Sweating Sickness (Colibacillosis)

Colibacillosis is caused by the bacillus *Escherichia coli* (see page 95). Young nestlings contracting the bacillus through infected food will become seriously ill, as the organisms can multiply almost explosively. Lack of hygiene in accommodations, dampness, and overcrowding can exacerbate the disease. *E. coli* infections are associated with severe enteric problems. Normally, the droppings of the young are contained in membranes, so that the parent birds can easily remove them from the nest. Unfortunately, the droppings of infected birds are watery and soon pollute the nest, causing sweating sickness. The warmth of the nest allows the bacteria to multiply even more. The bacteria can then gain entry to the yolk sac in the young unfeathered birds via the navel, sometimes through the skin, causing cysts at the site of infection, especially in the ear and throat region. The sick birds refuse to feed, weaken rapidly, and soon die, frequently on the fourth day after infection.

Colibacillosis is easy to detect by bacteriological testing and, as such an infection is quickly fatal, diagnosis and treatment must be immediate.

The name "sweating sickness" is remarkable. It came into being because of the fact that the lower part of the sick hen's body is wet, sticky, and rather dirty; the young are in a similar condition. A bird cannot perspire, as it has no sweat glands. The wet stickiness is caused by the foul droppings.

An *E. coli* infection should be prevented in the first place but if infected, the young birds should be sponge free of the infected fecal matter and dried off in a warm spot. Any diarrhea must be stopped as soon as possible to prevent dehydration. The whole family of birds should be placed in a clean, uninfected breeding cage. The old cage and contents must be cleaned thoroughly and disinfected and the fouled nest material preferably burned. Moving the birds may cause the parents to lose interest in the young, but hopefully they will continue to care for them. The risk taken is worth it if the disease can be cured. The disease can be treated with oral antibiotics, such as tetracycline or neomycin in the rearing food. Your avian veterinarian will be able to advise you on the correct treatment.

Humane Euthanasia

The very thought of having to euthanize a bird is a painful one, but there may, unfortunately, be occasions when it will be necessary. In cases of incurable injury or sickness, for example, it is often kinder to relieve a bird of its pain or misery than to prolong the inevitable. There are, of course, several ways of euthanizing birds in a humane and responsible manner.

Your veterinarian will select a method that is quick and painless.

The Canary Keeper's Medicine Chest

Though it is not recommended that the canary keeper have a veritable pharmacy, there are a number of pieces of basic equipment and medications that are useful to keep in store in cases of emergency.

Equipment

Heat source: Infrared lamp (60–100 watt bulb).

Hospital cage: Several commercial models are available, or you can make your own.

Thermometer: An easy-to-read environmental thermometer is essential for use in a hospital cage.

Cage covering: If you don't have a hospital cage, keep a selection of towels or small sheets for covering cages in emergencies.

Adhesive tape: A half-inch roll provides various uses, including splinting and so on.

Sterile gauze pads

Cotton-tipped swabs

Needle-nosed pliers and/or tweezers

Sharp nail scissors

Syringes or plastic eyedroppers

Medications

Maalox or Digel: For crop disorders. Eliminates gas and reduces inflammation. Dosage: 1 or 2 drops every four hours.

Karo syrup: For dehydration and as an energy enhancer. Add 4 drops to 1 quart (1 L) of water. Administer 1 or 2 drops of solution slowly into the beak every 20 to 30 minutes with an eyedropper.

Gevral protein: For loss of appetite. Always mix with Mull Soy, which is also a good source of essential vitamins and minerals. Mix 1 part Gevral with 3 parts Mull Soy. Tube-feed 1 to 2 ml, two or three times a day. Ask your veterinarian for details.

Kaopectate or Pepto-Bismol: For diarrhea and regurgitation. Soothes and coats the digestive tract; helps solidify the stool. Give 1 to 2 drops every four hours, administered with a dropper.

Milk of Magnesia: Relieves constipation, but is not suitable for birds with kidney or heart problems. Dosage: 1 to 2 drops in the beak from a plastic or glass dropper, twice daily for two days.

Mineral oil: For constipation, crop impaction, or egg binding. Administer 1 drop in the mouth per day for two days. Be very careful that the oil does not get into the respiratory system as it can cause pneumonia and vitamin deficiency.

Monsel solution or styptic powder: Use to stem bleeding, but do not apply near the beak.

Lugol's iodine solution: For massive thyroid enlargement (goiter). Half a teaspoon of Lugol with 1 ounce of water; place 1 drop of this solution in 1 ounce of drinking water daily for two to three weeks. See your avian veterinarian immediately.

Turpentine and petroleum jelly: For calcified feet or legs: Apply turpentine, then petroleum jelly to affected area daily for five days.

Betadine, Domeboro solution, A&D ointment, Neosporin, Neopolycin, Mycitracin, Aquasol A: For skin irritations. Neosporin, Neopolycin, and Mycitracin all contain antibiotics. Aquasol A is a cream containing vitamin A. All can be applied twice daily to the infected area.

If you want to learn about new developments in the field of avian medicine or to get in contact with an experienced avian veterinarian in your area, contact the Association of Avian Veterinarians, P.O. Box 811720, Boca Raton, FL 33481-1720. Telephone: (561) 393-8901.

Chapter Seven
Type Canaries

Since the first wild canaries came into captivity in the sixteenth century, the influences of housing, feeding, and selective breeding have led to the creation and perpetuation of many interesting, amazing, and attractive mutations. During the last century, Belgian, Dutch, and French breeders exploited almost every mutation that appeared in order to try to make something of it. Structural changes in the plumage and/or body were always of particular interest and eventually led to the recognition and standardization of local breeds of the various type canaries. Breeders in England initially were concentrating on the color varieties, but soon became interested in the changes in shape that were becoming apparent. Varieties included the large and sturdy Norwich canary, the smaller Gloster, the large Lancashire that may be with or without a crest, and the Scotch fancy, which with its high shoulders and half-moon shape always will attract much attention.

Another fascinating group are the frilled canaries, which have tightly curled feathers and long legs. A plunging decline in interest of type canaries at the end of World War II recently has seen a revival. The annual Paris show "La Nationale," organized by the Société Sérinophile et Ornithologique and held in December, is a sort of Mecca for type canary fanciers. Anyone interested in these birds should make an attempt to attend at least one show, if at all possible. Here one will see an absolutely breathtaking array of every conceivable kind of canary, and it makes one wonder how, in such a relatively short time, such an amazing selection of diversity ever could have emerged from a single wild species.

Special Housing

Type canaries generally are more delicate and cautious in their movements than color and song canaries. They really are unsuited to a large aviary, especially an outdoor one. The heavy plumage that some varieties have may help protect them against extreme weather conditions, but sooner or later they will succumb to moist conditions. Once the heavy plumage is wet, it takes a long time for it to dry out, and during this time the bird probably will develop a cold or worse. Even large, indoor aviaries are not really suitable for type canaries. Some of the larger varieties find it difficult to fly over greater distances, and even some of the smaller varieties have problems in a large aviary. A bird like a Gloster, which is supposed to be small and stocky, is likely to "grow out" too much in a large aviary and end up too long and rough. In a limited space, such birds hold their ideal body form much better. This does not mean, however, that these birds should be placed in tiny cages with barely enough room to turn around! A cage about 3¼ feet (1 m) long will give an ideal compromise size between a small decorative room cage and a large aviary. Do not overpopulate the cages; the more birds you place in a small cage, the more often it will have to be cleaned out to avoid soiling of the plumage. Also, the risk of disease is greater in overcrowded conditions and birds are more likely to become feather pluckers.

Normal breeding cage: The best accommodations for type canaries is the normal breeding cage: for small breeds (Gloster, lizard) a cage 16 to 18 inches (40–45 cm) long and deep, 18 to 20 inches (40–45 cm) high is adequate. For larger varieties (Yorkshire, Norwich) the cage should be at least 18 to 24 inches (45–60 cm) long, 16 inches (40 cm) deep, and 20 inches (50 cm) high. Such cages can be constructed in such a way that the end panels are removable so that longer cages can be made by standing them next to each other. Outside the breeding season, you thus can make ideal flights up to 10 feet (3 m) in length by standing five or six cages next to each other. Such a long cage will house 8 to 12 birds. Some males can get aggressive to others toward the breeding season, so it is often best to house these separately. Type varieties are best housed singly as the exhibition season approaches. This applies especially to the lizard and the frilled varieties, as these are more susceptible to feather damage.

Small areas and perches: A small space also helps keep birds calmer than when they are kept in a large, roomy aviary. In big areas, the birds fly away every time you enter, whereas birds in small cages cannot fly very far and tend to get used to the "boss" much quicker. Some fanciers force their birds to stay near the front of the cage by supplying perches only at the front. However, such perches must be cleaned and/or changed frequently as they soon get soiled. Such varieties as Gibber Italicus, Belgian Bult, and Southern Dutch frill, tend to quickly foul up the perches, due to their upright stance. In such cases, the perches should be changed at least every fourth day and the soiled ones thoroughly cleaned, disinfected, rinsed, dried, and sanded ready for reuse. You won't want to have birds with dirty feet and soiled tails! Some varieties use the tail to rest against the perch as a sort of prop to aid their awkward posture.

Another important point regarding perches is that they never should be set too low in the cage. The best position is just below half the cage height. Place two perches so that the birds can hop from one to the other. The distance between them is best if it is the same as that required in the exhibition cage for that particular variety. The next two perches are placed about 24 inches (60 cm) apart so that the birds must use their wings between the two points. In cages for Norwich and Yorkshire canaries, it is recommended that short 4½-inch (11.5-cm) perches be affixed ladder-wise against the back wall of the cage. In order to prevent squabbling, always make sure that there are adequate sleeping places in larger cages, so that each bird can reserve its own spot.

Breeding, Care, and Feeding

Cages and Nests

Small cages require regular cleaning and maintenance. Each year they should be cleaned thoroughly, sanded down, and repainted, so that they are easy to maintain hygienically for the next season. Floor covering can consist of mini corncob, clean silver sand, or pine bedding. Wood shavings or sawdust frequently is used, especially in England, The Netherlands, and Belgium. We personally prefer to use pine bedding. A good layer in the breeding cage, especially under the nests, functions as a shock breaker should an egg or nestling fall out of the nest.

Many type canaries require some assistance in nest building, especially varieties of frills. The Southern Dutch frill, for example, is apt to stuff the nest box so full of material that it cannot make a cavity. There is a great risk with this variety that the eggs will roll out of the nest. To prevent this, the fancier must make a suitable cavity in the nest.

Clipping

Before breeding some of the long-feathered varieties, clip away some of the feathers around the vent. The long down feathers of the Norwich, the Gloster, and the crested, for example, can interfere with fertilization. The feathers are best shortened with a pair of sharp nail scissors. Do not pull the feathers out, as first, it is painful for the bird, and second, they will grow again in a few weeks anyway. Also, do not clip them too short, as the hen will not be able to insulate the eggs in the nest. The shafts of short feathers also can be sharp during mating and thus interfere with fertilization. The ring of feathers around the vent must be left intact; clip only the down feathers.

Breeding Problems

Few problems should arise in the breeding of type canaries, especially with the smaller varieties. Glosters, lizards, borders, fife, fancy, and so on are not quite so productive as the color and song canaries. The larger varieties are even less productive, especially the Norwich and the Yorkshire. The frilled varieties usually raise a normal number of young, but here the larger ones also are less productive. The smallest frill, the Gibber Italicus, is an exception that frequently is bred to an almost lethal intensity; the consequences of this are obvious. Small nests and difficult rearing are problems that can be regarded as normal with this variety.

In general, it can be said that every variety of type canaries has its good and its bad breeders. It is the task of the breeder to build up a stud of canaries that are not only of excellent quality, but are good breeders.

Feeding

The feeding of type canaries is not too different from that of other varieties. Although it is frequently said that type canaries should be fed mainly on canary grass seed and oats, this need not be taken too seriously. It is a fact that this is the case in England, but we are not convinced that it makes the birds any larger. The reason behind this diet is more probably an economic one as these seeds are the cheaper in that country. One indication that a mixture of canary grass seed and oats does not make bigger birds is that this diet is also given to the Gloster, a variety that should be kept as small as possible.

The diet for type varieties is one that is adapted to a bird's particular needs. It must take into consideration the conditions under which the birds live. The amount of flying room and the ambient temperature are points that must be considered when you prepare your food mixtures. In a small, warm room, birds require less energy-giving food than in a large, cold aviary.

Seeds: Most type canaries are kept inside in relatively small cages and it is recommended that they receive a good variety of seeds. In the breeding season, the diet must be rich in proteins, to build up the bodies of the developing youngsters. Another important time is the molt; the birds require a good diet to replace the many, frequently long feathers that are lost. One must, however, take care with this feeding. The English breeds of Norwich, Border, and Gloster will quickly get too fat. It is therefore necessary to regularly inspect the birds and if they start to get too fat, the diet must be adjusted. A less energy-rich diet should be offered, especially in the rest period. Less energy-rich does not mean a monotonous diet; you must still see that your birds receive their necessary nutrients and vitamins.

Other foods: In addition to hard seeds, type canaries must regularly be offered egg food, green food, half-ripe weed seeds, and germinated seeds. But you must be careful: Too much green food, for example, can be dangerous for the Norwich canary; this bird is susceptible to digestive disturbances if it gets too much green or wet foods. You also should never *suddenly* give large amounts of green food or fruit. Gradually let your birds get accustomed to it, then you can give more. Some breeders of type canaries give their birds a handful of chickweed every day and get very good results. But these birds must be accustomed to the food from the time they are young.

Calcium: Type canaries must receive adequate calcium. Cuttlebone always should be available. Oyster grit is especially valuable for cages in which there is a mini corncob or sawdust floor covering. The grit should be offered in a separate dish. A mixture of oyster grit and mineral grit is especially valuable as it will supply both calcium and stones for the gizzard to help grind up food.

Baths

A daily bath is very useful for keeping type canaries in good condition. Fresh bathwater should be offered daily during suitable weather conditions—if the birds are kept in warm, indoor accommodations, the weather does not really matter. Soft water, especially rainwater, is the best kind as it has a gentle action on the plumage. Bathwater is best given in the morning and removed at midday so that the heavy feathers are dry before the birds go to roost. A daily bath for frilled canaries is not recommended especially as exhibition time approaches. The curly plumage of the frills is very sensitive to dampness, especially those feathers on the flanks, which are likely to straighten out if weighed down by water too often. Instead of bathing these canaries, they can be sprayed with a very fine, lukewarm mist spray; a houseplant sprayer is ideal for this. Do not make the bird too wet; otherwise, you will get the same result as too much bathing! A daily, light spray is sufficient, but use soft (rain) water where practicable. Once in their show cages, the only way to bathe exhibition birds is by spraying.

Competitions and Training

Show Cages

Type canaries kept in breeding cages as described will be better prepared for competitions than birds kept in large aviaries. They will be accustomed to movements close to them and will be much calmer. Moreover, the exhibition cage can be attached easily to the breeding cage—place the open doors together—so that the birds get used to entering it. If this is done well in advance of the competition, the birds will be more ready for it.

The bird used to the small exhibition cage will be much easier to train for competition than one that is placed suddenly in a small cage. A nervous bird will make a bad show specimen and there is also the danger it will panic and injure itself. A bird used to the show cage will only need to get used to changes in venue and the public. If the birds already are used to regular visits from family members and friends, this also will be a help, and the position of the cage should be changed regularly so the bird gets used to venue changes.

Therefore, a major part of preparing birds for exhibition is getting them used to an exhibition cage; some breeders even place the young in an exhibition cage shortly after they leave the nest. The parents still can feed the young through the wire.

Posture Training

Certain type canaries, such as the Belgian Bult, the Southern Dutch frill, and the Gibber Italicus, require further posture training. Although these birds should naturally take the correct posture, it may require refining. Bad posture in a type canary will lose points in exhibition. One way to getting birds to improve their posture is to suspend the training cage on a hook and spring, so that the cage moves about and the canary's perch moves like a branch in the wind. The bird will have to sit up straight and continually adjust its center of gravity. Its foot muscles will be strengthened and its posture should be improved dramatically. This should be done for no more than an hour a day as canaries are not particularly happy in moving cages.

Birds in show cages are best placed at eye level, but never less than 5 feet (1.5 m) from the floor. During competitions and especially the judging, the cages are placed at eye level. With frill canaries, the cages should never be set too close

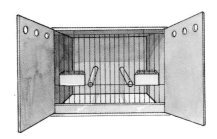

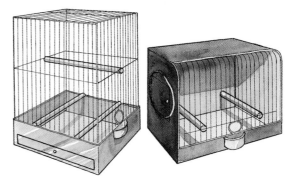

Various canary cages. Top: for singer; Bottom: for type canary (left) and an average show cage for color canaries (right).

to each other. There should always be a space of at least 2 inches (5 cm) between cages to prevent the birds from pulling each other's feathers out, an unfortunate habit that these birds have, if given the chance.

The Yorkshire and Lancashire are varieties that must have an upright posture. The posture can be improved after the birds are used to the show cage. The cage is placed in a container or covered with a board, paper, or similar covering that is so high that the bird has to stretch to its full height in order to look over the edge of the barrier. This method thus takes advantage of the canary's natural curiosity.

Birds with a curved or figure 7 posture require a different method of training. Such varieties as the Belgian Bult and the Southern Dutch frill must be taught to hold the head and neck horizontally. You can get them to do this by regularly scratching the underside of the cage. The noise will make them strain forward with the head and neck in a horizontal position to try to hear what is going on.

With all this training, one always should bear in mind that a bird will not do what it has not inherited from its parents. So one must be very selective and very patient. A careful breeding administration is very important so that faults are ironed out. A study of the required show standards will give one a good idea about what each variety should look like and how it should perform.

Type Canary Breeds or Varieties

(in alphabetical order)

Belgian Bult

This is one of the earliest varieties but its origin is not completely known. It probably evolved from the Mechelse waterslager as it has the typical arched (humped) back. It has been improved and refined by selective breeding.

This variety probably originated in an area of Belgium close to Ghent, Brugge, and Antwerp, and is supposed to have been perfected in about 1700. At that time it was called Grote Vogel (large bird), or Gentse Vogel (bird from Ghent). It became popular in England, where it was named the Belgian Bird. Thousands of the breed were sent to England, where, instead of perfecting the variety, it was used to help in the creation of new type canaries. It became so in demand for this purpose that Belgium suffered a shortage of breeding stock.

The high points in the history of the Bult were in the years 1700, 1840, and 1890. The two world wars took a heavy toll on the Belgian Bult and much valuable material was lost. An experienced fancier of type canaries once told us that he did not see Belgian Bults in Belgium or the Netherlands during World War II, just a few specimens in Spain. A few fanciers took care to preserve the race and today, thanks to Jan Dawans, who greatly promoted their popularity, there are again fanciers in the Netherlands and Belgium.

Bernese Canary

This variety is a national Swiss canary. Although it carries the name of the Swiss capital, it was not necessarily developed there. The Swiss have long been occupied in developing their own canary race (there is also a Swiss frill, which has been recognized in Germany and France in 1967 and 1968 respectively; it is still a scarce breed however), and they were not content until a bird had been produced that was as pure as the Swiss Alps themselves. This finally became the Bernese, a bird that stands tall and erect.

This variety probably was already in existence at the turn of the century because, by 1910 it already was well known in canary circles and, at this time, an official standard was drawn up. The Bernese has required many crosses and backcrosses for refinement. This variety came into the spotlight in an exhibition in Lisbon, Portugal, in 1966, when R. Koch showed a series of Bernese of very high quality. The breed now has enthusiasts in many countries.

Border Canary

As the name suggests, this lively, rotund, little variety was developed by fanciers on either side of the Anglo-Scottish border. As both the English and the Scots claimed the honor of developing the bird, it was named border canary in 1891 to keep everybody happy!

The original border canary was only a tiny 5⅓ inches (13 cm) in length and thus received the nickname of "Wee Gem." Over the years, the size has increased to 6 inches (15 cm). A drawing of the ideal border canary by N. Norman led to a standard being prepared in 1930. The well-known German artist H. Heinzel made a new illustration in 1968, which showed all details of size, form, posture, and so on. This is one of the easier varieties to breed; they will produce two to three broods of four to five young per season.

Columbus Fancy

This breed was developed by fanciers in America, especially Mrs. W. A. Finney. The name arises from the city of Columbus, Ohio, but the variety is popular all over the United States.

The Lancashire cobby, the Gloster fancy, the miniature Yorkshire, the border, and the Norwich plainhead have all played an important part in the development of the Columbus. The last two mentioned are definitely responsible for the crested gene. There are also plainheaded or smooth-headed Columbus canaries and this is fortunate as the best specimens arise from smooth × (bred with) crest, or vice versa, producing 50 percent of each type.

The Columbus fancy stands upright, with a very low angle across the perch but more vertically than the related crested canary. It is medium to large in size. Although most colors are acceptable, the leaning is toward a dark crest and a clear body. The color is a major point in judging.

Crested Canary

The first crested Mechelse waterslagers probably arose in about 1800. There is more certainty of crested Harz and Sakser varieties at that time. How the crest originated is somewhat of a mystery, though, because a canary is related to finches, so the tendency to have a crest is not altogether unexpected.

By careful selective breeding and the exploitation of appropriate mutations, the crest was developed and enlarged, probably with the use of the Mechelse waterslager. First came the crested Lancashire, later the crested

Norwich. Crossbreeding these two varieties further improved the crest and created the crested canary. Crested canaries occur both with and without a crest and the best results arise from breeding these together. The crested canary was developed by F. W. Barnett of Falkenham, Norfolk, England, in 1880.

Fife Fancy

This a small, agile, and popular (especially in the United Kingdom and Europe) rotund little canary, with a small, round head, a rounded breast, and a rounded back line with a half-moon-shaped tail inplant. The legs are short and the beak is somewhat pointed.

It was developed by mainly Scottish breeders who were trying to reduce the size of border canaries by selective breeding and ended up with the "dwarf" form. The name Fife is after a Scottish county and not a number (five) as is sometimes thought. It is the youngest variety among the type canaries—only about 45 years old—and was officially accepted in 1957, though the birds had been bred by fanciers for some time before that. It was in 1957 that the Fife Fancy Club was inaugurated in the Scottish town of Kirkaldy.

The most important point with the Fife fancy is its size—never more that 4½ inches (11 cm). Like the border canary, it often is referred to as "Wee Gem."

The Fife fancy is a good breeding bird, like most type canaries. All type canaries from 4½ to 5½ inches (11–14 cm) in length are good breeders. The breeding results are normally less successful with the larger varieties. This is a quirk of nature; the varieties that are closest in size to the original wild form generally are the best breeders. The easy breeding of the Fife fancy will mean that it soon will become very popular and a lot more of them should be seen in future exhibitions.

German Crest

This is really more of a color variety than a type canary. The greater part of the bird is like a color canary and it is only the crest that makes it a type canary. Color canaries with a crest have been known for a long time. The name German crest does not indicate the origination of the breed, only that it was the first type canary recognized by the Germans.

In 1963 the German crest was recognized by the German Canary Federation and the standard was accepted by the World Federation (COM).

The German crest is similar in body build to a robust color canary; sometimes the model is that of a waterslager as these are larger. The official size is the same as a color canary, namely 5½ inches (14 cm). The crest is somewhat less elegant than that of the Gloster. A good crest should be shaped something like a daisy. The center point should be as small as possible and round, never in the form of a stripe, a common fault with this breed. It should be nice and round and should cover the whole crown. Seen from the side, the crest should form a straight line just above the eye. The best birds have a crest that joins neatly at the back. If there is a parting in the feathers at the back of the crest, this is not a fault that will lose points, but there is a bald patch here in this breed that must be covered by the crest as much as possible

In the breeding of all crested canaries, the pairing crest × smooth is always recommended. The smooth-headed form of the German crest is a normal color canary, but one should make sure that it has a broad skull. The most common form is a red factor with a dark crest.

Gibber Italicus or Italian Humpback Frill

Belonging to the frilled type canary group, this variety is known on the continent of Europe simply as the Gibber. Although smaller, it looks identical in shape to the Southern Dutch frill, which, no doubt, played a part in its development.

Strangely, the Gibber is really the end result of erroneous breeding. The continuous breeding of intensive birds caused the feathers to become progressively sparser, until the breast and thighs ended up bald. The small size also can be blamed on the intensive factor. But it is the nakedness of the thighs and the breast that makes it a good Gibber Italicus. Usually it takes experienced fanciers to breed this variety, a certain insight and intuition is required

to know how far one can go with the intensive × intensive matings. Many young, unfortunately, are likely to die in their shell or just after hatching.

Giboso Espagnol

This frilled canary is one of the most recently recognized type varieties. It first was shown at the World Exhibition in 1982, in Roeselare, Belgium. It is similar in appearance to Gibber Italicus but a little larger and with a different posture. The Giboso stands straight on its stretched legs, holding its neck and head at an angle of 45 degrees. Unlike other frilled varieties, which are likened to a figure 7, this variety is more reminiscent of the figure 1. The head is carried so low that the beak almost touches the knees.

It is not yet known if this variety will be recognized officially by the COM. It must first prove over several years that it has become properly established. It also must be decided if it differs sufficiently from the Gibber Italicus to warrant new breed status.

Gloster

This is an interesting addition to the type canary group. It was developed by Mrs. Rogerson of Cheltenham (Gloucestershire, England) in 1925. Its popularity was enhanced by J. McLey, a Scottish show judge. It probably was brought about by crossing the Norwich with a small border and then selecting the smallest individuals for further breeding. Through constant selection, Mrs. Rogerson produced specimens that

Gloster canary.

were shown at the exhibition at Crystal Palace, London, in 1925. There are two types of Gloster: the Gloster Corona with a crest or crown and the Gloster Consort, which is uncrested. As crest × crest produces a 25 percent lethal factor, both types must be used for breeding.

Japanese Hoso

This is one of the smallest type canaries among the smooth-arched breeds. First examples of the race arrived in Europe in 1970, though they already were known in Japan in 1963. It was first officially recognized by the COM in 1974, but there were already many fanciers who took to the bird as a good breeding and show variety.

The Japanese Hoso could be taken as a miniature version of the Glasgow Don (the material from which the Scotch fancy arose). The most obvious characteristic of the breed is the half-moon shape, with the tail sticking under the perch, forming a clean curve with the body, which should be narrow and cylindrical. The shoulders are narrow and barely wider than the fine, long neck. The head is narrow and "snaky" and must be carried well forward to complement the total curve of the bird, but should be held not lower than the shoulders.

The long wings should lay comfortably along the body and the unforked tail should complement the overall, half-moon shape. The thighs should be visible and the legs should be held slightly bent, not straight. The plumage should be as smooth as possible, but in view of the shape of the body, this is not wholly possible.

The size of the bird is one of its important points. The recommended length is 4⅓ inches (11 cm), but up to a maximum of 4⅔ inches (12 cm) is acceptable.

Preparation for exhibition is similar to that of the other type canaries. One must see that the birds already use the half-moon stance in the training cages. Only birds that already have a tendency to the posture should be used. Other birds are unsuitable as they never can be trained to take on the correct stance.

The Japanese Hoso is a good breeding bird and should produce average results. With good pairings, one can allow two broods a year without problems, but that should be the maximum. A third brood from these little birds is less likely to be altogether successful and will tend to exhaust the parents. Usually smaller, intensive specimens of 4⅓ (11 cm) are selected for breeding, but this is somewhat risky as these small birds show all the faults in their short plumage. Sparse feathering on the thighs and bald patches around the eyes are the first signs that the intensive (non-frosted) factor is too strong.

Too much inbreeding, as is the temptation to produce smaller birds, also is not recommended. The best results seem to come from intensive × grizzled or half-intensive × half-intensive and ensuring a strict adherence to size and shape.

Japanese Hoso.

Lancashire

The ancestors of the Lancashire canary most probably would have been brought to England in the eighteenth century by Flemish and Dutch weavers. The Lancashire is known to have been used frequently in the development of other breeds, such as the crested and the Yorkshire, around 1870. These crossings, unfortunately, led to a deterioration in the quality of the Lancashires, which thus soon lost popularity. During World War II, the Lancashire was all but lost altogether. All of those seen today are "reconstructions" developed from the very varieties that were developed from the Lancashire in the first place. Although the present-day Lancashires are still not exactly common on the show benches, their popularity is certainly on the increase.

The Lancashire is the largest of the English type canaries, with a minimum length of 8 inches (20 cm) but specimens of 9 inches (23 cm) are standard. It is a stately and proud, upright-sitting bird. At first sight it seems to have some of the points of the Yorkshire, but close inspection will show many differences. The neck is longer and thicker than that of the Yorkshire, whereas the breast is rounder and fuller.

The important point of the Lancashire is its horseshoe-shaped crest. It begins behind the line of the eye, forms a three-quarter circle around the front, and the center is in the center of the head. At the back of the head, the plumage should align as smoothly as possible with that of the back, giving the impression that the crest is only on the front part of the head. This looks its best when the crest is the same color as the rest of the body, and a dark-colored crest is thus not favored in the variety.

The smooth-headed Lancashire is the same as the crested with the exception of the head, which should be wide and fairly long. The eyebrows should be prominent and hang along the eye. The head plumage should be soft and abundant, but must not stand up behind the eye. Selective breeding should be carried out to maintain the length of the body and quality of the crest.

Lizard Canary

When the Huguenots fled from France to England at the end of the sixteenth century, they brought their pets along with them. One of these was a particular type of canary that eventually developed into what is known as the lizard. One of the oldest type varieties, this breed underwent few changes in its first 400 years. Once extremely popular, it became quite scarce during World War II—a survey carried out by the English magazine, *Cage Birds*, came up with a mere 30 pairs.

A very intensive breeding program has since greatly increased the number of individuals, and this splendid variety is now quite common. It is set apart from other canaries by its spangles, said to resemble the scales of a lizard, from which the name obviously arose. This marking effect is due to the fact that the feather tips are without color until after the juvenile molt.

As the canaries age, the colors at the edges of the feathers will become broader and spoil the attractiveness to some extent. The beak, legs, wings, and tail should be black. Agate brown and isabel lizards also exist. There are also secondary colors, such as the nonintensive yellow with the ordinary lizard, the intensive golden yellow with the gold lizard, the white with the blue lizard, and the red factor with the bronze lizard. Although some regard the lizard as a color or color-marked canary, it is, according to the COM, at least partially a type canary.

Milan Frill

The Italians have tried to create their own race with this variety, which, as its name implies, originated in Milan. However, it is so similar to the Parisian frill, that a separate description is barely necessary; the small number of differences should suffice. Even the standard descriptions are almost identical.

This fairly recent breed was developed to form a connection between the type and color canary fancies. Contrary to most other type canary breeds, which are judged on form, posture, and plumage, the color plays an important role in the judging of this breed.

A combination of the many colors of the color canaries with the interesting shapes of the type canaries should, in theory, provide some astoundingly attractive birds. Unfortunately, in practice this does not quite turn out as one would like it. For a start, the type canary fancy is relatively young in Europe and America, and there is much work to be done in maintaining and improving the type canaries before one should really think about introducing too many color variations. By introducing the blood of color canaries into relatively recent type races, there is the danger of causing a deterioration in standards. Care therefore must be taken with experimentation. It sounds good to have type canaries in all sorts of colors, but the end results could be fatal for the type canary fancy.

There are really only two differences between the Milan and the Parisian frill; the first is the color. The Parisian does occur in many colors, but the most common are the green, the yellow, and the green variegated. The Milan is a self-colored bird, and variegated specimens cannot be recognized as Milans. For a long time, the Milano Bianco (White Milan) was the only known color frill but now the clear red-orange and the self-blue also are found. Other colors are not yet officially recognized. A Milan frill thus can be described as a Parisian frill without variegation, in the colors white, clear red-orange, apricot, and self-blue.

A second small difference to the Parisian frill is in the size. The Milan must be a minimum of 7⅓ inches (18 cm); the Parisian, a minimum of 7⅞ inches (19 cm) long.

It has been ascertained that the Milan is a good breeder and raises its young better than the Parisian. However, the breed is seen infrequently on the show benches. Perhaps it is the combination of good form and plumage of the type canary and the pure color of the color canary that makes it difficult to produce enough suitable birds for exhibition purposes.

Muenchener

This German variety is not seen much in the United States, but in its homeland it is quite important. It does, however, appear regularly in many world exhibitions. The cause of the Muenchener's sparse popularity could be the fact that it is not so clearly a separate breed. All four of the birds of the type group are similar to each other. Only the top birds of these groups are easily recognizable, but all the in-between, mediocre individuals can give breeders and judges great problems in deciding to what breed they belong. It is thus quite possible that the ancestors of the Muenchener include the Belgian Bult and/or the various frills.

What is known is that the oldest Muencheners had frilled plumage. Its greatest popularity was probably between the years 1920 and 1930 when it was already a smooth-plumaged bird and was bred for form and color. Since then, the Muenchener lost popularity for many years, but in the last ten years has again become increasingly important.

In body build, the Muenchener can be compared favorably with the

Belgian Bult and the Scotch fancy, but there are naturally a number of differences. It is fairly small and varies in length from 6 to 6½ inches (15–16 cm). It has a very fine body, its breast must not be too wide but full, so that the breast line sticks roundly out. This is contrary to that of the Scotch fancy, where the line of the breast should go slightly in. The shoulders should be as narrow as possible. The back is only lightly curved with the main curve at the shoulders. The bird should sit upright on its perch so that the lower part of the back and the tail are vertical.

The head is fairly small and slightly flattened; the neck is long and thin and carried at an angle of around 45 degrees to the imaginary line drawn from the shoulders to the legs. The joint of the neck and body must follow a flowing line. The principal characteristic of the Muenchener is thus the straight, sloping neck with the straight back. The legs are relatively long and must be clearly bent, thus not so straight as those of the Bult or the Scotch.

Northern Dutch Frill

Like the Gibber Italicus, the origin of this race is also rather obscure. However, the experts believe there is a great possibility that the frilled varieties were first developed in the Netherlands. The following passage on the subject comes from Eugène Legendre, an old member of the Comité Ornithologique International:

"The Dutch laid the foundation for the frilled canaries. Their first interests were concentrated on the area of selecting long-feathered canaries. Through these long feathers, which originally were concentrated mostly on the breast and soon started to fall somewhat open, a comparison to Dutch national dress was obvious. From the drawings we were given to examine, the feathering on the back and flanks also became thicker, not so much in the form of curls but more like a scoop. The breeding of this variety spread to Belgium and then to the northern areas of France, especially in Roubaix and even further south to Picardie, where the Frill was named 'Roubaisien' and 'Picardien.' Later he was named the Northern Dutch Frill. If we delve further into the history of this frilled variety, we will see that the breeding of this bird went as far south as Paris, where the Parisian Frill was then developed." (From a letter to the authors.)

Norwich Canary

This variety probably originated in Flanders and came via Belgium to Britain, where it was further improved in Norwich, hence the modern name. Old illustrations show that it was very similar to the waterslager, which was probably one of its ancestors. This old race was considered a color variety for some time. The lizard canary may have played a role in this, as the lizard definitely was crossbred, as evidenced by the silky and shiny feathers of the Norwich.

According to the illustrations, the Norwich canary underwent various changes around 1800, so it is likely that the original type goes back to well before this.

A large exhibition in honor of the Norwich canary was held in Norwich, England, in 1890. About 400 entrants are said to have participated! At this event the standards for the breed were set, along with a scale of points for form and position. The color was no longer thought to be a major factor and the bird became a type rather than a color canary. With interruptions only during the two world wars, the Norwich has been a very successful breed with a second form (crest and crest bred) also becoming popular.

Padovan Frill

This is another Italian creation that is very similar to the Parisian frill. However, there are a few characteristics that set it apart, the most obvious being the crest. The bird is somewhat smaller than the Parisian, but must always be at least 7¼ inches (18 cm). The frills also may be a little shorter. Another difference is in the collar, which must be nicely rounded and conspicuous, but the feathers are not so long and the whole collar sits lower than in the Parisian. The Padovan frill should have a well-developed crest that should not be compared with that of the Gloster; it is larger and hangs partly over the eyes. Also, it need not be so neat as that of the Gloster and is influenced by the frill feathers.

The color of the crest is also rather important. Like the Milan, the

Norwich canary.

Padovan must be self-colored, and variegated specimens are not acceptable. The crest may, however, be another color, preferably darker than the body. A dark crest on a white or yellow body is ideal for this variety.

There is also a smooth-headed form of the Padovan frill. The main difference between these, the Milan and the Parisian, is the rather smooth plumage above the collar. The fact that it is a crest-bred bird must be visible in the Padovan; this is indicated by the obvious eyebrows.

Parisian Frill

Some real giants of the canary world are found among this breed. Some of these have tail feathers that alone measure 5 inches (12 cm). Very little is known about the origin of the Parisian, though it is thought to have descended from certain Dutch varieties, including the Northern Dutch frill. The Parisian frill was refined in the region of Paris, France, and a society for the breed already existed in 1867. It is an attractive variety, robustly built, and with tightly curled frills arranged symmetrically on the proud, semierect body.

Scotch Fancy

Little is known about the origin of this breed. Earlier versions were known as Glasgow fancy or Glasgow Don. In all probability, the Belgian Bult had a lot to do with its ancestry, and the hooked form of this breed developed further into a semicircular shape. Other ancestors are anyone's guess. Perhaps the Southern Dutch frill also played a part?

Southern Dutch Frill

Strangely perhaps, in spite of its name, this variety originated in southern Italy, especially in the regions of Naples, Caserta, and Benevento. It probably inherited its

Scotch Fancy.

high back from the Belgian Bult and its frills from the Northern Dutch frill. As mentioned earlier, this variety was probably an ancestor of the Gibber Italicus. As far as it is known, the Southern Dutch frill made its first appearance in about 1920 and reached its peak just before the outbreak of World War II.

It is a well-proportioned bird with the figure 7 shape almost perfect, and its head shape is much like that of a lizard. It is a rather nervous breed that often cannot stand still during exhibitions. Fortunately, this typical behavior is allowed for in the scale of points. Sadly, this breed has become quite scarce recently and the available breeding material is somewhat inbred. If an improvement could be made, this fascinating frill certainly would make a comeback.

Swiss Frill

This variety is not seen very often in the United States, or indeed in Europe outside its native land. As its name suggests it was developed in Switzerland, probably from a mixture of the frill canaries available at the time. It is a relatively old race, though the first official recognition was in 1968 when the standards were fixed at the COM congress in Paris.

It is a so-called light frill, meaning that the curled feathers occur only on certain parts, in this case, the mantle, the breast, and the flanks. The mantle feathers should cover roughly two thirds of the back, should end in a straight line, and should hang symmetrically on each side of the body. The flank feathers should be well developed as in the Southern Dutch frill. The breast frill feathers are shorter than in the Dutch frills; they must start away from the wings.

The head and neck are smooth and the bird is about 6⅜ inches (16 cm) in length. The main difference between the Swiss and the Dutch frills is in the posture. The Swiss also stands on stiffly erect legs, but the body is held in the form of a half moon. The head is held forward, but not held deeply as in the Southern Dutch. The tail is held against the perch.

The Swiss frill is not the easiest of varieties to breed. They do not make good parents, especially the younger individuals. This is probably one reason why they are not seen often on the show benches. The correct, half-moon shape of the bird also is difficult to achieve and must be carried out by very careful selective breeding. However, there are a few dedicated fanciers who are working hard on the variety and it could perhaps have a bright future.

Yorkshire

This is probably the favorite English canary and is aptly named the gentleman of the fancy. It is indeed a proud and impressive bird which is said to have been shown first in Yorkshire, England, around 1870. Bradford seems to have been the headquarters of the bird, which originally was intended to have an improvement on the Lancashire. The

Swiss Frill.

variety was developed from three main breeds: the Belgian Bult, the Lancashire, and the Norwich. It took some time to develop it to the desired standards, which was not achieved until about 1935.

For breeding, the Yorkshire requires a large cage and a relatively large nest box or pan. It does not breed as easily as perhaps the border or the Gloster, but if good care is taken, two nests of three young can be expected per season. More than three young in a nest is undesirable, as they must grow very quickly in the first weeks. It is also best to breed with well-matured (two-years

Yorkshire canary, a real champion!

old or more) parents, which will produce more and larger young than younger pairs.

Feeding Yorkshires also requires special attention so that the young grow well, as they need a great deal of protein in the development of the long wing and tail feathers. Each breeder usually has a favorite menu, but the following seed mixture should be adequate: 10 parts canary grass seed, 4 parts rape seed, 4 parts rolled oats, 1 part niger seed, 1 part hemp, and 1 part linseed (flax). Additionally, a little lettuce and/or poppyseed may be given, often sprinkled over a little soaked bread. The English often give their birds thistle seeds, usually soaked, as it is a particularly hard seed. Green food always should be given, but sparingly.

Conclusion— Judging Show Birds

There are other type canaries, but these are too scarce or obscure to really be of concern. A few remarks regarding the judging of show birds will be of value.

One of the first points to bear in mind is that all birds entering an exhibition should be in top condition and prime health, should be trained to be bold and proud, and should be able to display the correct posture for the variety in question. Type canaries are very dependent upon judging, which has the inherent danger of the birds becoming "victims" of their keepers' experiments. All breeders should be thoroughly aware and respectful of the requirements and standards of type canaries. A small amount of knowledge also can be as bad as no knowledge whatsoever, with some breeders attempting to correct imperfections that are not imperfections at all. In so doing, they may introduce even more undesirable characteristics.

A good example of this is the well-known case of introducing Norwich blood into the border, in order to give it a "heavier" look. This never should have been done. The border is a small type canary and such a cross also brings with it black brows

Key for Type Canaries

- Category A: Frilled Canaries
  1. Parisian frilled canary
     Color frill
     Badouaner
  2. Northern Dutch frill
  3. Southern Dutch frill one-colored
  4. Swiss frill
  5. Gibber Italicus
  6. Padovan frill
  7. Milan frill

- Category B: Posture Canaries
  1. Belgian Bult
  2. Scotch fancy
  3. Muenchener
  4. Japanese Hoso

- Category C: Form Canaries
  1. Border fancy
  2. Raza Espagnola
  3. Norwich
  4. Yorkshire
     Continental type
     English type

  5. Bernese canary
  6. Lancashire
  7. Fife fancy

- Category D: Crested Canaries
  1. Gloster
     Corona
     Consort
  2. German
     crested
     noncrested
  3. Crested canary
     crested
     crest-bred

- Category E: Marked Canaries
  1. Lizard
     silver
     yellow
     red
     clear-capped
     broken-capped
     noncapped

and filled necks, undesirable traits for the border. Glosters, also, are frequently muddled in with the crossing of color canaries. In order to maintain good type canaries, such practices must be avoided.

The show judges' job, therefore, is to be very strict and selective and to award low marks to any birds of less that top quality. The chart above shows the COM key for type canaries.

Chapter Eight
The Miracle of Genetics

Color-bird Canaries

A fancier who has proceeded past the beginner stage and has gained some good experience in the general care and breeding of canaries most likely will want to advance to more ambitious projects. However, many beginners with only a vague knowledge of genetics and color breeding often are astounded by what is unexpectedly produced by a pair of birds they have mated together. This is why it is necessary to learn at least the basics of genetics—the science of heredity—if you wish to control the colors and types of birds you are breeding.

Cells, Chromosomes, and Genes

You quite probably will be aware of the fact that animals and plants are composed of living building blocks known as cells. Each of these cells is so small as to be invisible to the naked eye, but viewed through a microscope, they are extremely interesting to study. There are different cells for different functions in the body, but the simple basic cell consists of a cell wall, enclosing a nucleus surrounded by plasma. Growth in living things occurs through a process of cell division (mitosis). At a given moment, the cell constricts roughly across its center, dividing nucleus and plasma, and gradually tearing itself apart until it becomes two little identical cells, each with its own wall, plasma, and nucleus. These little cells absorb nourishment, grow to a certain size, and divide again, thus together allowing the growth of the whole living organism, in this case the canary—or shark, or snake, or oak tree, or human being—that contains billions of cells.

Almost every new multicelled organism is derived from a female and a male parent, each parent donating a cell: an egg cell from the mother and a sperm cell from the father. These two cells fuse together to form a single cell, which is called a zygote. The zygote is the first cell of the new life and it begins to grow by cell division.

In these two donated cells that fuse to form the zygote must lie all of the characteristics of the new being.

In the case of the canary, this includes its color, its form, its quality, its circulatory system, its digestive system, its respiratory system, its bones, its feathers, its shape, and even its temperament. These characteristics are contained in the chromosomes, which themselves form part of the cell nucleus. These chromosomes are the carriers of life itself and are the organizers of bodily makeup. The chromosomes can be seen only through an electron microscope, and within them are even smaller bodies called genes. It is these genes that define the inherited characteristics. They decide the color of a bird or, in humans, the color of your hair or your eyes. They decide a whole lot of other things and are thus the ultimate deciders of life itself. A cell always has a certain number of chromosomes, and always an even number. Each time a cell divides, the chromosomes also divide so that two cells contain the same number of chromosomes.

The only exception is the zygote, which is formed by the fusion of the egg and the sperm cell. In this case, the egg and the sperm cell (the sex cells) each carry only half of the normal number of chromosomes found in every other cell of the donor parent. The canary has, for example, 42 chromosomes in all of its cells, but only half that amount (21) in its sex cells. This means, of course, that the zygote formed from the two parent sex cells again will have 42 chromosomes and thus be the start of a new canary!

Recessive white.

Every new canary is formed from half the genetic makeup of its mother and half the makeup of its father. So, one can have a perfect canary cock, but if this is mated together with a less than perfect hen, you cannot expect the young to be perfect. Some of the bad points of the hen can turn up in the youngsters, and mask the perfectness of the father. An experienced breeder, therefore, will use only good cocks *and* good hens.

Mutations

You now can apply this knowledge of cells, mitosis, chromosomes, and genes to the wild canary, from which all domesticated canaries are descended.

As F. Van Wickede noted, the wild canary is a grayish color. And, since they were all the same color, all the hens and cocks bore the same-colored young.

If you examine the gray color of a wild canary, you will find it to be a mixture of brown and black pigments

Non-frosted brown canary.

over a yellow base color. Some canary breeders speak of "three coats on top of each other," which together give the gray color. These three coats are inherited by the young from their parents, and providing nothing goes wrong, the same color will perpetuate from generation to generation.

Fortunately (for the canary fancier at least), something occasionally does go wrong, and this is called a *mutation*—a sudden genetic change in a gene or genes. The cause of this, in most cases, is not known, but it is known today that some mutations can arise as a result of the sex cells of an animal being subjected to radioactivity of one sort or another. There are other possibilities and one can, for example, produce mutations with certain chemicals, or with X-rays.

A mutation resulted in the yellow canary, when for some unknown reason, two of the canary's three coats (the brown and the black)

were lost, leaving the plain yellow undercoat. Do not imagine, however, that such dramatic mutations are a common occurrence. Certain tiny, unnoticeable mutations may happen all the time, but big, vivid, exciting ones, like the first appearance of a yellow canary, are very rare indeed. Reasonable mutations are estimated to appear once in every 400,000 canaries! However, that number of birds is bred in many countries every year, so there is a good chance of *some* mutations appearing annually.

Most mutations are of no use to the breeder of canaries and, in many cases, they are not even noticed. They do not necessarily alter any outward color or form, but may affect internal organs, for example. The mutations important to the canary breeder are those that affect the color of the feathers and, to a lesser extent, the general shape of the canary and its plumage.

In this connection, consider another example. Blackbirds are renowned for being black; that is why they are called blackbirds. Blackbirds almost always produce black babies as well, but very occasionally, a blackbird with white flecks, or even a completely white blackbird hatches from an egg.

Through a fault in the genetic inheritance, part or all of the dark pigment in the blackbird has been lost. In the latter case, the bird is an albino. If only one element of the pigment is lost (the black), an isabel color will result.

One easily can understand how important mutations have been in developing all the different breeds of canaries. Breeders also can use mutations to their great advantage in improving varieties. Mutations are essential in developing completely new colors and shapes. By crossing one mutation with another, still more varieties can be produced. And so it goes on; theoretically there is no limit to the number of varieties one can have, providing the mutations continue to turn up on a regular basis.

Through the loss of the black and the brown pigments, the yellow canary came about, but the yellow canary itself has many more possibilities; in the first place because it was much more attractive than its gray relatives, but also because it has more genetic possibilities.

In summary, note the following:
• Mutations mean new color varieties.
• Selection opens the way for better specimens.
• Crossing of mutations produces even more color varieties.
• More colors can be produced by hybridization; thus, the red-factor canary got its red color via the hooded siskin.

Recessive and Dominant

Every breeder of birds or animals needs to be familiar with the terms *recessive* and *dominant*. These terms are used frequently and are important to the result of crossings. There have been whole technical books written about these terms, but what the breeder needs to know is not difficult.

A dominant color is, unlike a recessive color, always visible. In place of color, characteristic also can be used, as recessive and dominant can apply to other inherited factors. These terms also can be applied to humans; in general, for example, one can say that dark-haired and brown-eyed people are dominant over blue-eyed blondes and that heavy, rounded noses are dominant over small, tilted noses.

In canaries, the color is the most important aspect of these terms. In nature, the original color of wild birds is always dominant over color mutations, so gray is always dominant over yellow.

In practice, this means that a gray mated to a yellow will produce gray young, the yellow being concealed or hidden. Similar examples can be found in zebra finches. The natural color of these birds is gray, and this

Frosted gold satinet.

gray is dominant over other colors. If you cross a gray zebra finch with a white one all the young will be gray.

It also can be said that the dominant color is always the *visible* one, and the recessive color is always repressed by the dominant one. However, the bird still has the recessive colors, because it has half the genetic makeup of each parent; they just cannot be seen.

Indeed, if a gray cock canary is crossed with a yellow hen, the result will be all gray young, as the gray is dominant. But gray young will have inherited the yellow factor from the mother, and will be able to pass this (invisible) color onto their young. Such birds also are called gray split for yellow or simple gray/yellow. Gray is the visible and yellow the invisible color, which can be passed on to the next generation.

Frosted ivory gold.

Homozygous and Heterozygous

Homozygous (pure) and heterozygous (split), two terms important to the bird breeder, are closely connected with dominant and recessive.

A homozygous or purebred bird possesses only the genes of its visible color. The original wild canary is such a homozygous bird. It has its gray color—*and nothing else*—and is not able to pass any other colors on to its offspring. The yellow canary, which arose from the loss of the brown and black pigments of the original bird, is also homozygous or purebred, as it possesses only the yellow (lipochrome) color and nothing else.

Earlier in the text, it was noted that the young arising from a crossing of a gray × yellow will all be gray, but they also have the invisible yellow color. These are gray split for yellow or heterozygous.

There are, in fact, relatively few numbers of homozygous canaries. Canaries have been domesticated and interbred for such a long time that to find a homozygous gray canary is extremely difficult. Moreover, you cannot see what you are looking for; only the dominant color can be seen, and not the colors that are hidden. It is necessary to actually breed the bird to find out what it is.

There also will not be many breeders who can supply you with homozygous birds of any color, unless they have kept a comprehensive studbook over many generations of breeding.

It is unfortunate that it is so difficult to obtain homozygous birds. If one wishes to concentrate on particular colors, it is preferable to have some homozygous birds of that color available as then one will know that the offspring will be the right color. With nonpure birds, it always will be a gamble as to what colors one finds in the nest.

To summarize:
- *Recessive*: the hidden factor.
- *Dominant*: the visible factor.
- *Homozygous*: pure, passing on only the outward color and nothing else to the offspring.
- *Heterozygous*: split, capable of passing on other, invisible colors to the offspring.

Yellow Canaries

The homozygous yellow canary came into existence when a mutation lost the brown and black pigments in the plumage, leaving the yellow lipochrome (a fat-soluble dye that colors the feathers). Mated together, light yellow birds produced light yellow offspring. Another mutation arose during these breedings, the dark yellow. If a light yellow and a dark yellow bird were paired together, the young were a mixture of light yellow and dark yellow, producing the intensive yellow bird. This intensive factor is dominant over the light yellow and intensifies the yellow lipochrome. Intensive × intensive is a mating that should not be tried as it will bring

Blue recessive.

out the lethal factor; in other words, the young will die in the egg or shortly after hatching.

Light yellow × dark yellow will produce light yellow if the offspring inherit this factor from both parents, dark yellow (intensive) if the offspring inherit light yellow *and* intensive, and dead young (lethal factor) because both parents may pass on the intensive factor to some of them. The rules of heredity for light yellow and dark yellow are:

Light yellow × light yellow = 100% light yellow

Light yellow × dark yellow = 50% light yellow and 50% dark yellow

Dark yellow × dark yellow = no offspring (lethal factor; do not attempt this mating)

Note: In all crosses, the convention is to identify the cock first.

Citron
The citron is really a yellow canary that is affected by the so-called

Dimorphic red-orange.

Citron × citron = 100% citron
Citron × noncitron = 100% intermediate citron

Intermediate citron × intermediate citron = 25% citron, 50% intermediate yellow, and 25% noncitron

Intermediate citron × citron = 50% citron, 50% intermediate citron

Intermediate citron × noncitron = 50% intermediate citron and 50% noncitron

White Canaries

There are two kinds of white canaries: the dominant white that originated in Germany, and the recessive white that originated in England.

Dominant White

This variety is heterozygous: thus its inheritance parallels that of the ordinary yellow canary. As it tends to push the yellow into the background, the white is considered dominant. The effect is not complete, however, as there is always a hint of yellow left at the curve of the wing and on the outer edges of the primary flight feathers. Although this yellow never has been bred completely out of the birds, good show specimens reveal as little of it as possible. If two white canaries are crossed together, the yellow color will be enhanced and there is even a good chance of 25 percent yellow, as both parents carry the yellow factor and pass it on to their young. The heredity rules are:

intensive blue optical factor. There is, in fact, no blue color present at all, but the feather hooklets are of a shape that reflect light in such a way as to deceive one's eyes. As blue and yellow make green, so this blue reflective light combines to produce an apparent green sheen in the bird's plumage.

Heredity of the blue factor is recessive and intermediate—between dominant and recessive; a crossing between a white and a red snapdragon will produce pink flowers. The intermediate inheritance can be proven by crossing a citron with a light yellow canary. The offspring will be a shade between light yellow and citron, with the blue factor barely apparent. The heredity rules are as follow:

Dominant white × dominant white =
25% yellow, 50% dominant white, and
25% lethal factor (since intensive ×
intensive brings out the lethal factor)

Dominant white × yellow (any shade) =
50% dominant white and 50% yellow

Recessive White

Being recessive by nature, a recessive white crossed with a dominant yellow, for example, will produce visibly yellow offspring but with the hidden white factor; in other words, they will be yellow split for white or yellow/white. Heredity rules are as follows:

Recessive white × recessive white =
100% recessive white

Recessive white × yellow =
100% yellow/white

Recessive white × yellow/white =
50% yellow/white, 25% yellow, and
25% recessive white

Recessive white × white/yellow = 50%
recessive white and 50% white/yellow

Albinos

The white varieties have lost the pigment in their plumage but are not albinos, as they still retain the pigment in other parts of the body such as the eyes, beak, and feet. In the albino, *all dark pigment is lost*, giving us the "pink" eyes (the pink color being the blood vessels) and a total absence of lipochrome. The bird is thus pure white in appearance. The beak is a light horn color, almost transparent, and the pinkish tinge to the feet and toes is due to the blood vessels showing through the scales.

Color Canary Varieties

A great many color varieties of canaries have arisen through mutations, selective breeding, and even hybridization over the years. The birds lacking the dark pigments are known as the lipochrome group because they still possess the lipochrome, which is an evenly distributed, smooth-textured yellow or red coloring substance. (Pigment has a rougher texture.) Varieties of the group include:

Light yellow	Ivory
Dark yellow	Pastel
Citron	Red
Dominant white	Red-orange
Recessive White	Orange
Dimorphic	Apricot

Red-orange agate.

Non-frosted (red-orange) bronze.

The second group includes the pigmented birds that are further split into four groups (see below).

In addition to those listed, there are ranges of pigmented dimorphics, opals, pastels, and inos. Some fanciers may object to these groupings. Many may feel that the agates, isabels, frosteds, pastels, opals, and inos should fall into the brown series, because they possess the same pigment but are enriched with yet another factor.

Brown Canaries

A normal canary has black and brown pigments plus lipochrome in its plumage. Lose the black pigment and what remains is a brown color, which still masks the lipochrome—only visible if both dark pigments are lost. The first so-called brown mutation appeared around 1700 and it soon became referred to as feuille morte (dead leaf) due to its similarity to the leaves in the fall.

This must have been an exciting time for canary breeders as this mutation was used in the origination of many other colors. A brown canary has red eyes, as the black pigment is missing for them. How-

Green Series	Brown Series	Agate Series	Isabel Series
Self-green	Gold brown	Gold agate	Gold isabel
Gold green	Silver brown	Silver agate	Silver isabel
Citron green	Red-brown	Red agate	Red isabel
Bronze green	Red-orange brown	Red-orange agate	Red-orange isabel
Orange bronze	Orange brown	Orange agate	Orange isabel
Green			
Red-bronze			
Blue			
Steel blue			
Slate blue			

ever, the brown pigment is still present so the eyes are much darker than the pink of the albino. The brown color is homozygous so that brown × brown produces 100 percent brown offspring. It is also sex-linked in its inheritance, not dominant or recessive.

The original brownish gray of the feuille morte has long since been modified and most browns today are more of a chocolate color. Really dark specimens are referred to as maximal brown.

Sex-linked Inheritance

The sex of all animals is also determined by chromosomes and genes. One of these chromosomes, with its supply of genes, possesses a single sex characteristic, whereas there is another with double sex characteristics. The sex chromosome usually is referred to as the X chromosome. The cocks have the double X (XX) chromosome and the hens the single X (XY). When young are born, about half of them will inherit one X chromosome from the male and one X chromosome from the female, making it a young male. The other half will inherit the X chromosome from the father and the Y chromosome from the mother, thus making them females

Breeders, of course, have no say as to how many cocks and how many hens they will get from a par-ticular mating; it will depend on the potluck of how the X and the Y chromosomes fall into place, though it is always the hens, with their XY chromosomes, that determine what the sex of each offspring will be. Strangely, in mammals, it works precisely opposite: It is the males that have the XY chromosomes and the females the XX chromosomes, thus it is the former that will determine the sex of the offspring.

Color

Not only the sex of an animal is decided by the genes in the chromosomes, but also other characteristics, including color, for example. However, if some of these color characteristics are connected with the sex chromosome, they can be regarded as sex-linked color factors. In such a case, the visible color is thus bound to the sex of the animal and with some particular matings one can tell the sex of some offspring by just looking at the color.

In canaries, melanin is one of these sex-linked inherited colors. The melanin consists of black and brown pigment, both of which are also sex-linked inherited. In order to appear brown, the cock canary must have the double brown gene. If he only inherits a single brown gene, he will not appear brown but he will have brown in his genetic makeup and thus will be capable of passing it on. A hen need have only a single brown gene to appear outwardly brown. This means that there are no brown inherent hens, an impossibility.

This also goes for all other pigment hens, which can inherit only their own outward color, unlike pigment cocks, which not only can inherit their outward colors, but also invisible colors. In other words, hens are always homozygous to their pigment colors but cocks also can be heterozygous to their pigment colors.

Pigment birds are canaries that, in one form or another, possess the green canary ancestry and include the agates, the brown, the isabels, and the pastels.

These are placed in this order because the question of dominance arises. The natural color is dominant over the agate, the agate over the brown, the brown over the isabel, and the isabel over the pastel.

This dominance must, of course, be taken into consideration for breeding. For example, a brown homozygous cock paired to an isabel hen will produce brown hens, as brown is dominant over isabel.

The brown hen offspring are homozygous, as no brown heterozygous hens are possible, but the brown cocks from this mating carry the isabel gene and are thus heterozygous. This means that the hens can pass only the brown color on to their offspring, but that the cocks can pass on brown or isabel.

Thus the rules of inheritance for brown canaries are a follows:

Brown cock × brown hen =
100% brown offspring

Brown cock x normal hen=
50% normal/brown cocks and
50% brown hens

Normal/brown cock x normal hen = 25% normal/brown cocks, 25% normal cocks, 25% normal hens and 25% brown hens

Normal/brown cock × brown hen =
25% normal/brown cocks, 25% brown cocks, 25% brown hens, and 25% normal hens

Normal cock × brown hen =
50% normal/brown cocks and
50% normal hens

A closer look at these rules indicates that normal cocks and normal hens refer to birds that do not have the brown factor. They can have any other color, as long as they do not have the brown factor in their makeup. In most cases, one can see if the birds possess the brown factor, but never forget that cock birds can possess the brown factor in its hidden form. Of course, if you have kept a good studbook, you will know exactly what to expect from your

Fife canaries.

matings as you will know whether cocks are normal or split. However, taking cocks ad lib and hoping for particular offspring is a very hit-and-miss affair, until birds are known for several generations.

With regard to the rules, split hens are not mentioned as, of course, they do not exist. They can be only wholly brown or not brown at all. You will notice further that brown hens appear three times in the rules, but brown cocks only once. If the first rule (brown × brown) is included, this ratio will become 4:2. In practice, this means that it is easier to breed brown hens than brown cocks, as the odds are smaller.

For curious fanciers with not much patience, breeding with the brown factor is to be highly recommended. They do not need to wait until the birds are fully grown before they know what sexes they have. If, for example, they pair a brown cock with a green hen, they will know from the second inheritance rule that all the brown offspring will be hens and all the green offspring will be green/brown cocks.

The brown cocks and the brown hens are homozygous and can pass on only brown. The green offspring of the above pairing are heterozygous cocks as they can pass on the brown factor as well as their visible green color.

What if the curious fancier reverses the pairing and mates a green cock with a brown hen? According to the fifth rule, all of the young will be green, but the cocks will be split for brown. Although mainly brown and green canaries have been discussed, the same rules naturally apply to agates, isabels, and pastels.

Other Varieties

Brown (Feuille Morte) and Citron

Brown (Feuille Morte Jonquille)

A good brown canary must have an even coloration, with the wing color as close as possible to that of the rest of the body and all on a light yellow background. Stripe effects show a strong tendency to appear, especially on the back, but these are not favored and every attempt should be made to breed them out by strict selection. The frosted factor is also common, but there is no objection to this (see later in the text).

The citron brown canary (feuille morte = dead leaf; jonquille = greenish yellow) possesses the blue factor that also can be seen in the citron yellow canary. The variety is not considered to be very attractive and is not so popular today. A double citron factor, however, can produce some quite stunning results. These have a deep brown tail and wings with a lighter shade on the belly. The breast is a greenish brown haze. Stripes on the back or elsewhere are frowned upon, as is any black color.

The bill and the feet are lighter brown. If a single brown factor is used, the offspring take on too much green and will not do well at shows. The citron yellow canary often is used to improve color and strength in the blue canary.

Gold Brown Canaries

The intensive double yellow factor provides the opportunity to breed beautiful birds that will draw a great deal of attention at exhibitions, especially if they show a little of the frosting factor.

The breast and belly are a light, golden chocolate brown. By using a maximal brown bird and a double yellow factor canary, the offspring will be beautiful. The main brown color will contrast admirable with the secondary golden yellow color. Maximum main color should be used in breeding so this is passed on to the young.

Intensive and Frosted (Nonintensive)

It is easy to understand the word intensive, as applied to canary breeding, if the common yellow canary is used as an example. Such a bird has clearly visible variations in its shades of coloration. The breast and rump, as well as the crown, are usually a deeper and more intense shade than the wings, flanks, or tail. A good yellow canary should be equally strong in color over its whole body. This can be achieved by introducing the double yellow factor to give the offspring more lipochrome. In examining one of the not so evenly colored canaries, it is

noticeable that the short feathers are more intensively colored than the long ones. This means that although the lipochrome is distributed evenly among the feathers, the long feathers have to make do with the same amount as the short ones, thus losing color intensity. The answer to this is to try to breed birds with shorter feathers so that the shades are more evenly distributed.

One danger of this is eventually producing birds that are sparsely feathered. It is therefore necessary to follow a sort of middle-of-the-road pattern in order to produce the desired results. A nonintensive bird has larger feathers and thus has more room for the same amount of coloring, often resulting in almost an absence of color in the feather tips and a total absence in the outer hooklets, giving the bird the so-called frosted appearance. The intensive bird, on the contrary, has shorter feathers with the same amount of coloring making a more evenly distributed yellow. The frosted factor is rather difficult to get rid of, so many breeders exploit it, producing birds that are evenly frosted all over. Frosted × frosted produces a progressively stronger frosted factor, whereas intensive × intensive produces an almost double intensive factor. These crossings are not advisable.

Green Canaries

The pied green canary possesses the yellow lipochrome as well as the black and brown melanin. A vague frosting is often present, but this is usually acceptable. Stripes on the back, however, are undesirable. The most attractive birds can be bred from pairs where the frosting factor is minimal, or from a pied green × slate blue or gold green canary, which will minimize the stripes on the back. Heavy dark striping on the back is known as maximal pigment and can be minimized by following these heredity rules:

Maximal pigment × maximal pigment = 100% maximal pigment

Maximal pigment × minimal pigment = 100% maximum/minimal pigment

Maximum pigment × maximum/minimal = 50% maximal pigment and 50% maximum/minimal pigment

Maximum/minimal × maximum minimal = 50% maximum/minimal, 25% maximal pigment, and 25% minimal pigment

Minimal pigment × minimal pigment = 100% minimal pigment

The gold green canary is also a pigment bird, getting its appearance from a double yellow factor and a double blue factor. Extremely attractive offspring can be produced from a crossing of gold green normal intensive to gold green with a weak frosting character. The following crosses also produce attractive offspring: gold green × citron green, gold green × gold isabel (also with gold agate), and gold green × silver brown. Gold green × gold agate often is done to increase the small amount of black marking, but such a cross produces less-perfect gold isabels and gold agates with single

blue factor, so one needs to be very selective in order to avoid problems further down the line.

The citron green canary possesses the single yellow factor, giving greater leeway to the blue. Citron green × brown produces very beautiful offspring.

The Silver Brown Canary

White combined with pigment produces the silver factor; thus a pairing of a dominant or recessive white with black or brown melanin will produce the silver factor. The silver brown has a background color of recessive white; white being the best background.

The best results are obtained from normal brown × silver brown, preferably with a single yellow factor and a weak frosting factor, but it is necessary to avoid too much green in the makeup. The popular cross of silver brown × gold brown is not recommended because of the resultant green sheen that silver brown young will inherit.

The Blue Canary

Blue canaries are, in fact, green with the dominant white and the blue factor. The blue factor is a structural color, but needs to be quite intense in the blue canary.

The citron yellow canary relies on the blue factor to give it a greenish sheen. With dominant white, the sheen is much stronger, so that the green combined with the white gives us a slate-colored blue canary. If the blue factor is doubled, the result will

Getting to know each other.

be steel blue. The frosting factor should be kept out as this will diminish the blue effect. The best blue canaries are produced using the intensive factor and avoiding the introduction of brown.

Good pairings for slate blue offspring include slate blue × citron green (with only a slight accentuation of the intensive factor and minimal pigment), and citron green × silver isabel or silver agate. For steel blue offspring, the best matings are steel blue × gold green and steel blue × citron yellow, the former probably being the best. The steel blue canary must have the intensive factor, though not too strong a strain. Frosting must, of course, be avoided altogether.

Agate and Isabel

These varieties are both mutations caused by the so-called paling factor, which lightens the pigment.

Being sex-linked, this factor means that only cocks can be split for agate or isabel, never the hens. The rules of heredity are as follows:

Agate cock × agate hen =
100% agate offspring

Isabel cock × isabel hen =
100% isabel offspring

Agate cock × nonagate hen =
50% nonagate/agate cocks and
50% agate hens

Isabel cock × nonisabel hen =
50% nonisabel/isabel cocks and
50% isabel hens

Nonagate/agate cock × agate hen
25% agate cocks, 25% agate hens,
25% nonagate/agate cocks and 25%
nonagate hens

Nonisabel/isabel cock × isabel hen =
25% isabel cocks, 25% isabel hens,
25% nonisabel/isabel cocks and
25% nonisabel hens

Nonagate/agate cock × nonagate
hen = 25% nonagate/agate cocks,
25% nonagate cocks, 25% agate hens
and 25% nonagate hens

Nonisabel/isabel cock × nonisabel
hen = 25% nonisabel/isabel cocks,
25% nonisabel cocks, 25% isabel hens
and 25% nonisabel hens

Nonagate cock × agate hen =
50% nonagate/agate cocks and
50% nonagate hens

Nonisabel cock × isabel hen =
50% nonisabel/isabel cocks and
50% nonisabel hens

These rules show that agate and isabel are passed on to the offspring; the following combinations will produce lesser results:

Nonagate/agate cock × agate hen

Nonisabel/isabel cock × isabel hen

Nonagate/agate cock × nonagate hen

Nonisabel/isabel cock × nonisabel hen

These matings produce cocks that are split and therefore not distinguishable from pure agate or isabel, which are more desirable for breeding. The agate and isabel factors can be introduced to all pigmented birds but, of course, not to lipochrome birds.

Agates and isabels are classified into the following groups:

Agates: light yellow agate (agate), gold agate, citron agate, silver agate, orange agate, orange-red agate, red agate intensive, and frosted red agate.

Isabels: light yellow isabel (isabel), gold isabel, citron isabel, silver isabel, orange isabel, orange-red isabel, red isabel intensive, and frosted red isabel.

Agates Lacking the Red Factor

Pigmented, pied green canaries have a yellow ground color, with brown and black melanin added. If the agate factor is introduced, the agate (light yellow agate) canary will be produced. A good example of such a bird has a base color of light yellow, covered with an ashy gray; there should not be any brown in the color, but a frosting factor is permitted. The best results arise from pairing agate with a weak intensive factor and light yellow ground color to isabel with a weak intensive factor and light yellow ground color. As the offspring receive the "paling" factor from both parents, they will have a beautiful light shade. Stripes should be as few as possible, which is why pairing agate to agate should be avoided.

A good gold agate has a double yellow factor and an absence of frosting. A weak strain of intensive can be introduced to keep the feathers short and in good color. Gold agate × gold isabel usually will produce the best results.

Citron agates should be evenly colored and this can be maintained by using the blue factor. It should be light gray, without a trace of brown. The use of a moderate intensive factor is best for this variety. The best results will be produced from citron agate × citron isabel.

Silver agates are produced by pairing agate and slate or steel blue, and the actual color of the variety is influenced strongly by the blue factor. There are two possibilities: lead gray (single blue factor or no blue factor) and pearl gray (double blue factor). There should be absolutely no trace of brown in either type.

Beautiful offspring will be produced from silver agate × silver isabel. The former should have minimum pigment for best results.

Isabels Lacking the Red Factor

The normal (light yellow) isabel should have a minimum of stripes,

The hooded siskin male can be crossed with the canary hen and produce the red factor coloring.

used in order to avoid greenish hues. Really beautiful offspring can be produced by pairing a silver isabel with a slight intensive factor to an agate with a single yellow factor.

The Red Factor

The red factor was introduced into the canary by pairing it with the red siskin, a bird that naturally has red in its plumage. This red coloration is a kind of lipochrome having some qualities in common with the yellow lipochrome of the canary. The red factor can be used as an undercolor for pigment canaries or to determine the coloring of lipochrome canaries.

Red-Orange Bronze and Frosted Red-Orange Bronze (= Nonintensive)

These are bronze green birds with a red-orange (intensive) undertone, producing a yellowish bronze color. Bronze green intensive × bronze green (both having a good red-orange undertone) is probably the best pairing. Pairing with parents also possessing a fairly heavy frosting factor will produce frosted red-orange bronze offspring.

Red Bronze and Frosted Red Bronze

The best offspring will be produced by pairing red bronze with frosted red bronze. The undertone is intensive deep red. The frosted red bronze possesses a light frosting

which are narrow and short. A cinnamon color is superimposed on a light yellow background. By introducing a weak strain of the frosting factor, some excellent birds can be produced, the best arising from light agate × isabel. The citron isabel, which possesses a blue haze, often is used with the isabels to deepen the color of the flight feathers.

A gold isabel should have no stripes if used for exhibition purposes. A good specimen will have some degree of the intensive factor, which shortens the feathers and deepens the color. A double yellow factor should be used for best results and the frosting factor preferable should be left out. A pairing of gold agate and gold isabel also will produce lovely offspring, providing both parents have a minimum of a light intensive factor.

The silver isabel has a fine, light silver gray chest and flanks and a darker back with not too heavy stripes. The blue factor should not be factor, making it somewhat duller on the back.

Orange Brown and Frosted Orange Brown

The orange brown is produced from a combination of brown and intensive orange but is only considered good if it has short feathers and there is no frosting factor present. Intensive orange brown × lightly frosted orange brown will produce the best young. The frosted orange brown differs from the orange brown, in that it has longer feathers and the normal frosting factor. Best results will be obtained by pairing lightly frosted orange brown to lightly frosted orange brown.

Red-Orange Brown and Frosted Red-Orange Brown

The red-orange brown has an intensive orange brown undertone and the primary color is brown. Stripes are present but must be kept to a minimum. Best results will be achieved from red-orange brown with a light frosting factor × red-orange brown with a light intensive factor.

The frosted red-orange brown has a moderate frosting factor that must be evenly distributed throughout the plumage. The best results for this variety will be obtained by crossing red-orange brown with a light frosting factor to a similar bird.

Orange Agate and Frosted Orange Agate

To produce the first variety, you need to start with a bird that has an even orange undertone, short feathers, a not too heavy intensive factor, and no frosting factor. Thus, a cross between an orange agate with a moderate intensive factor and an orange isabel with a weak frosting factor will produce the best orange agate offspring. The frosted variety will have longer feathers and will require both parents to have had the frosting factor.

Red-Orange Agate and Frosted Red-Orange Agate

This variety should have a smooth and even red-orange ground color. Only a limited amount of striping should be present and any brown on the back or chest is most undesirable. It should have agate marking on the flanks. The frosted variety must have an evenly distributed frosting factor. The best offspring will be produced from orange agate with a moderate intensive factor mated to a red-orange isabel. Both parents should have a light frosting factor for the frosted variety.

Red Agate and Frosted Red Agate

A good specimen of the red agate will have an even red undertone with agate. The wings and back should be deeply colored and should not have any brown. Best results are obtained from red isabel × red agate, preferably when one partner has a not too accentuated intensive factor, the other a weak frosting factor. For frosted specimens, both parents must possess a weak frosting factor.

Orange Isabel and Frosted Orange Isabel

The undertone of the orange isabel is orange overlaid with a weak isabel factor. Its feathers will be quite small as it possesses a weak intensive factor. The orange color should be as evenly distributed as possible with no paler patches in the plumage. The pigment should be clearly visible, but brown is out. A fairly weak intensive orange isabel crossed to an orange agate with a small degree of frosting will produce some very fine offspring. As usual, the frosted variety needs both parents to have a light frosting factor.

Red-Orange Isabel and Frosted Red-Orange Isabel

The two most important requirements for the red-orange isabel are a minimum of pigment and a lovely red-orange undertone, without too

Frosted red-orange male agate.

many heavier or lighter-colored areas. There should be a clear, but very fine, striping on the back. The short feathering results from the fairly weak intensive factor. Brown should be totally absent and pale areas are undesirable.

The best red-orange isabels will be produced from pairing a red-orange isabel with a fairly weak intensive factor to a red-orange agate hen that has a light frosting factor. The frosted variety should have both parents with a very light frosting factor.

Red Isabel and Frosted Red Isabel

The red color should be evenly distributed and shades of brown, or paler areas, are undesirable. Although a minimum of isabel should show, it must be readily apparent. The best red isabels will be produced by crossing a fairly light intensive red isabel with a lightly frosted red agate, or the other way around. Frosted individuals must have both parents with a light frosting factor.

Apricot

There are two types of apricot, the red-orange with frosting and the red lipochrome, which also possesses frosting to arrive at the apricot color. Too much frosting, however, will reduce the quality of the white color and cause the feathers to become too long. The best apricots arise from crossings of intensive red (or red-orange) to red-orange (or red) with a weak frosting factor.

Intensive Orange

No frosting factor is allowed in the intensive orange, and the intensive factor must also be weak. Evenly distributed over the body, the orange color looks very good on the short feathers. Pale spots anywhere on the body or limbs are not allowed, nor is the blue factor. The best offspring will result from a normal intensive orange × weakly frosted bird.

Red-Orange Intensive

It is difficult but desirable to remove the brown from the plumage of this variety. Pale quills are also a problem. The red-orange color should be evenly distributed. The best young will be produced from red-orange × red-orange with a weak frosting factor.

Red

There should be no yellow undertone in the ideal red canary, whereas the red itself should be evenly distributed. Pale patches are most undesirable, as are frosting and the blue factor. The most successful matings seem to be intensive red × red with a weak frosting factor.

Dimorphic Canaries

The red siskin contributed the dimorphic character to color canaries and also introduced the phenomenon of sexual dimorphism in canaries. (Dimorphism is the difference in the appearance of sexes; for example, the great visual difference between a peacock and a peahen.) The dimorphic factor is sex-linked, but the characteristics of this factor only become visible after the first molt. The best heredity rules to follow are:

Dimorphic (or nondimorphic/dimorphic) × dimorphic

Dimorphic × apricot

Dimorphic × frosted red-orange

Dimorphic × frosted red

In the last examples given, a sex-linked heredity will appear, so it is best not to use reverse matings; for example, frosted red × dimorphic.

Pigmented Dimorphic: It is possible to introduce the dimorphic factor to all pigmented varieties. It is best, however, to keep to the following mating: dimorphic (or pigmented dimorphic) × pigmented dimorphic. To arrive at pigmented dimorphic, pigmented dimorphic × lipochrome dimorphic is used. Some of the lovely color varieties include dimorphic bronze, dimorphic agate, dimorphic isabel, and dimorphic brown.

The Pastel Factor

The pastel factor reduces the intensity of pigment, particularly the black melanin. It is sometimes referred to as the "paling" factor. It can be introduced into the pigmented birds providing they possess red or yellow lipochrome.

A green canary that has a first reduction or paling factor is an agate

Recessive silver satinet.

in a similar manner, whereas the brown pastel shows a much reduced brown also due to a reduction in the brown melanin.

In the pastel canary, the ground lipochrome remains unchanged and the actual pastel color is a result of the combination of the lipochrome and the reduced pigment. This could be compared to a box of water colors; if brown is mixed with white, the result is beige and if a little red is added, a reddish beige is produced.

The reduced pigment color in green pastels is grayish; with the agate pastels it is blue gray, the brown pastels beige, and the isabel pastels a very light beige.

canary. If it receives a second reduction factor, a green pastel will result. The difference between these two birds is that the green agate appears the color of burnt peat, through a reduction of the brown melanin; the green pastel, however, possesses a second reduction factor that mainly affects the black pigment, reducing the number of melanin grains and spreading them out. This results in the striping, which is mainly caused by the black melanin in pigment canaries, being much more limited. The color of the green canary is thus reduced and has a tendency to become brownish.

The agate pastel is produced by a second reduction factor in addition to the one that brought about the agate. The isabel pastel is produced

The Ivory Factor

This mutation arose in about 1950. It causes a change in the structure of the feathers by increasing the thickness of the keratin layer in the hooklets. These hooklets, which affix themselves to the barbules, are devoid of any color. In normal canaries, the yellow lipochrome is located in both the barbules and the hooklets, but the ivory canary has it only in the barbules, thus reducing the strength of the color. In addition, the thicker layer of keratin reduces the visibility of the color, giving the ivory impression.

The ivory factor can occur in both light and dark yellow birds and thus will vary itself in shade. It also can be introduced to both pigment and lipochrome canaries, though in the former, the pigment plays no role in the determination of the color of the ivory. The ivory factor is also sex-linked; in other words there are no nonivory hens split for ivory, only cocks. The ivory factor occurs only visibly in the hens.

The Opal Factor

Opals are semiprecious stones with a translucent, milky white appearance, through which many colors may shine. These colors seem to be gleaming from the interior of the stone.

A canary mutation, which first appeared in Germany in 1949, was given the name "opal" by its breeder long before it became recognized as such. It did indeed take a long time before show judges would accept the opal as a variety in itself and then only after intense selective breeding had refined the color. In fact, good opal canaries are still scarce.

The opal is a very interesting mutation that has a good future in the canary fancy. It arose through a change in the arrangement of the barbs in the feathers. If you look at a section of a barb under high magnification, you will notice that it consists of four layers. The outer, horny layer encloses the cortex, which has a core, in turn enclosed by a transparent wall.

Normally, the melanin, the black and brown pigments, are found in the cortex and mainly the outer side, making the feather darker on the outside than the inside. Canaries with the blue factor have melanin also in the core.

In the opal canary, some melanin also occurs in the core, but the rest of it is "reversed." It is mainly on the *inside* of the cortex resulting in the feathers of an opal canary being darker on the inside than the outside. The light falling from above reaches the darker pigments in the inside parts of the feathers, thus showing the colors as if viewed through a milky glaze, as is the opal gemstone.

With plain pigment in the opal variety, the color appears to be bluish gray as most of the light is absorbed. The blue light waves are distributed through the walls and makes the color bluish gray.

The light absorption in the core and in the inner part of the cortex is so strong in the opal canary that the brown pigment is no longer visible and the opal is thus sometimes referred to as a "brown inhibitor." The brown inhibition is so strong that pastels and isabels with the opal factor show hardly any pigment in their feathers. Even the brown opal shows hardly any pigment and striping is totally absent. Brown opals are beige in color with a bluish sheen from the presence of the blue factor. This all means, of course, that opal factor birds with the most black melanin will show the deepest pigment in their feathers. Comparing a gold green canary with a gold green opal reveals that the latter shows deeper color and more blue that the former.

The yellow and red lipochromes are, of course, normally used in opal canaries, as they do not influence the core of the barbs, only the cortex.

By breeding in the ivory factor, factors that inhibit and weaken the brown pigment are introduced. If this combination is used with the red factor, a red canary with obvious blue factor will be produced. This gives a violet-red color, which makes good future possibilities, as the secrets of the opal factor are further researched.

The first requirement of opals is that the opal factor must be clearly visible. In practice, opals hardly *appear* to have the black or the brown factor. Opals with a white ground color produce the blue opal; with a yellow ground color they produce the gold. The opals are reces-

Hybrid European Goldfinch x Canary

sive-inheriting, that is, the color is visible only if the young inherit the factor from both parents. Thus, opals can be bred from two nonopal/opal canaries.

Opals should have pigment color in the deep, visible blue factor and as little frosting factor as possible.

The Inos

Jean Hervieux, in a book that appeared in 1712, mentioned white canaries with red eyes—probably albinos. F. Van Wickede also mentions albino canaries in a book published in 1795, saying that they were weak.

It is a fact that albino canaries have appeared several times over the years, but they have disappeared again, probably because they are too frail. In a genuine albino, the pigment should be totally absent—not as in the white canary, which still has pigment, as can be seen from the dark eyes and the color in the feet. Genuine albinos have fiery red eyes as the red blood vessels can be seen through the lack of pigment.

The albino canary that is known today is not a genuine albino, and there is some confusion in the bird fancy with regard to this bird. Of course, pleasure is derived from such a bird, but there is some disagreement over its name. Perhaps this question can be solved if one does not take the view that they are like budgerigars with sex-linked inherent albinos, lutinos, and rubinos. But

Fourteen-day-old hybrid (Canary x Serin).

then the question remains as to how one should deal with the pigmented red-eyed birds.

The term "ino" arose in Belgium to describe the red-eyed factor. That is perhaps understandable as it places the albino question in middle ground and discussion can include white ino, yellow ino, red ino, gold isabel ino, silver agate ino, and so on. For the nonpigmented birds, the names albino, lutino, and rubino remain.

It is not known who bred the first inos, but they are certain to have arisen in Belgium where they were developed by various breeders, probably around the year 1964. It also is not definite if the first inos arose from gold isabel × gold isabel. However, the inos are now here to stay, wherever they came from.

The fact that many of these inos belong to the pigmented group, shows that inos are not necessarily influenced by the albino factor. The so-called albino and lutino canaries are therefore not to be likened to the

sex-linked inherent lutinos and albinos that are known among the budgerigars. The ino factor in canaries is a special factor, not related to albinism. There is also never any thought of sex-linked inheritance, but from a totally unrelated recessive factor. Like the opal and the recessive white canaries, mother and father must pass on the ino factor for the offspring to be ino. The rules of heredity for ino canaries are:

Ino × ino = 100% ino

Ino × nonino = 100% nonino/ino

Ino × nonino/ino = 50% ino and 50% nonino/ino

Nonino/ino × nonino/ino = 25% nonino, 25% ino, and 50% nonino/ino

---

One can see that the rules are simple enough and that with an ino and a couple of nonino/inos, one can achieve interesting results.

With the lipochome group of canaries, there are no possibilities. It is possible to breed the ino factor into white, yellow, and red lipochromes to produce albinos, lutinos, and rubinos. The last is a new name derived from ruby (thus, ruby red).

Phaeos

These birds have no stripes or dark-colored feathers. The phaomelanin along the feather edges thus shows as a checkered pattern on the back. The stronger the brown, the darker the pattern. The eyes are ruby red.

The Parisian Frill comes in two groups—the erect type (erige) and the horizontal position (grenouille).

The Satinet

This relatively recent mutation has more or less obvious back and flank markings. The pigment has not developed in the edges of the feathers and these are thus white. The lizard, the color canary among the type canaries, has an attractive checkered pattern that can be compared to the scales of a lizard. Enterprising breeders have paired the lizard to the satinet, to produce a new color—the pearled canary. The number of possibilities are almost endless.

Possible Crosses with Wild Songbirds

A number of potential crossings between canaries and other species follow. Most of the offspring will turn out to be infertile hybrids, or mules, but some very attractively colored birds can be produced:

Canary × greenfinch
Goldfinch × canary
Greenfinch × canary
Yellowhammer × canary
Linnet × canary
Redpoll × canary
Siskin × canary
Scarlet rosefinch × canary
Alario finch × canary
(especially dominant white)
Black-hooded red siskin × canary
Black-head siskin × canary
Cape canary × canary
(especially with gold agate)
European canary × canary
(Gloster Corona)
Greenfinch × canary (Gloster)
Mexican red sparrow × canary
(Yorkshire)
Mozambique siskin × canary
(especially dominant white)

Chapter Nine
Song Canaries

Song Versus Call

Almost every bird has a song or at least a voice and there is no real distinction between the *song*—for attracting a mate, maintaining pair bond and territory, stimulating breeding behavior, and so on—and the *call*—for distress, aggression/intimidation, and so on. In most cases, a song is distinguished from other bird utterances by its complexity in the number and combination of notes. The circumstances that cause a bird to sing are more or less correlated with the reproductive cycle. The voice box of a bird is not situated in the upper part of the windpipe as in humans, but deep in the breast cavity at the point where the windpipe, or *trachea*, divides into two *bronchi*. The inner wall of the voice box, or *syrinx*, carries a number of membranes that vibrate with the expulsion of air from the lungs, thus producing the sound, which varies tremendously from one bird species to the next. The air channel in the syrinx can be varied in size by opening and closing with special muscles. The syrinx is often different between the sexes and, in most cases, the cock bird has a much greater song repertoire than the hen, though the birds with monotonous songs, such as crows, the syrinx is similar in both sexes.

The quality of the song depends not only on the structure and ability of the syrinx, but also on the *mood*, which can be influenced by environmental conditions. Each bird has the urge to song its own "folk song," but young nightingales allowed to grow up with other songbirds will mimic the songs of their foster parents. If they are reared among other kinds of songbirds, including nightingales, however, they still seem to prefer to learn the song of the nightingale.

The length of the airpipe varies greatly from species to species and the number of tracheal cartilaginous rings in a raptor (bird of prey), for example, is 30, compared with 350 in the flamingo. The trachea is even longer than the neck and may reach into the breastbone. The structure of the syrinx plays an important part in bird classification, and the so-called passerine or songbirds, which include the canary and almost half of all the world's 9,500 or so bird species, have an advanced type of tracheobronchial syrinx operated by seven pairs of special muscles.

Heredity

Attracted by the quality of the canary's song, its ability to mimic, and the ease with which it could be bred, the Germans (especially) of the Harz Mountains and of the province of Saxony exploited the bird's natural talents. Special automatic musical instruments were manufactured, which mimicked the voice of the canary—and these were played continuously to young cocks until they also had mastered the song. These canary breeders soon realized that each bird had its own talent, and also its own particular tone. Birds with the most mellow or musical tones were selectively bred to produce cocks with even better songs. Some of those with the best songs were then used to train young cocks, so that the talent could be used in two ways. Indeed, some of the birds were sold exclusively as trainers, others as songsters.

Professor van der Plank of the State University of Utrecht, the Netherlands, was one of the first to clearly state the possibilities of inheriting song characteristics among canaries:

"The canary's singing talent is inherited, though there are other factors, such as the individual anatomical structure of the respiratory organs and the gullet, which may also influence the quality of the song."

"There is also an inherent 'song intellect' in canaries. In this respect, the canary is gifted with understanding. The singing urge or singing ardor is also inherent."

On the anatomical build of the singing apparatus, the length of the vocal chords, the width of the vocal cords, the elasticity of the connection with the main gullet, the diameter of the breast cavity, and the form and circumference of the lungs and crop all have a direct connection with inherited factors, whereas the type of notes or tones have an indirect connection.

The sounds that are emitted by a "plain" canary, obviously come from the vocalization structure, the syrinx, and are not of the desired quality, though such a bird can bring forth full tours of proper length and harmonious order and can be considered to have *intellect* of song. Canaries that sing only three or four tours, and thereby often emit sharp flute tones and fluid like bell rolls, are failing the necessary organ structure as well as the intellect. *A first-class singer must have a combination of a*

Wooden song canary cage.

good singing organ (syrinx) and a sure amount of intelligence!

Both factors are inherited and are the key for the breeding of good song canaries. Unfortunately, the structure of a bird's internal organs are not visible, so that it is impossible to say if a bird has a good or not so good singing organ structure by looking at it. This is not necessarily an obstacle to building a line of song canaries, but it is technical in that the hen canary can give no indication of how good the singing factors are. These can be found out only after the birds have produced young.

Waterslager canaries.

Training Young Song Canaries

It is not difficult to breed canaries, but to produce fine, prizewinning singing canaries is a question of expertise, dedication, and ongoing enthusiasm. If there are no demands with regard to the quality of the canary's song, things are quite simple, as every cock canary sings and this may be adequate to please its owner.

Fanciers and breeders of song canaries, however, regard the singing talent of their birds with great importance and develop this in their stock whether it be Harz, rollers, or waterslagers. They must spend a great deal of their free time doing this.

Every young cock canary must be trained before he becomes a useful and calm singer. The training begins during the breeding in the nest and continues in the singing cage.

The major rule at the beginning of training is the separation of the sexes; the young cocks thus must be placed in a separate cage or aviary so that their singing is not disturbed by the hens. For good song development, they should be kept where they cannot hear the hens, but not everyone has enough room to do this. The fancier divides the aviary into three flights—one for the young cocks, one for the young hens, and one for the old breeding hens. Some very good old cocks are used as training birds in the flight with the young cocks. At first, the young cocks will make a veritable cacophony of short, unrelated rolls and flutes, wherein the experienced breeder will not be able to pick out many straight tours. (A tour is a complex series of rolls and flutes linked by harmonious transitions.) The young birds do not sing all day, depending on such circumstances

as the position of the aviary, sunlight, type of strain from which the birds arise and so on. In general, the singing periods lie between 8:00–10:00 A.M. and 3:00–5:00 P.M.

To prevent the birds from putting each other off during the singing, a sing study perch is erected in the aviary. This consists of a number of equal-sized, short pieces of board, spaced about 6 inches (15 cm) apart and through which a ½-inch (1.5 cm) perch passes; the boards touch the roof of the aviary, thus forming a number of compartments, each large enough for a single bird to sit without seeing its neighbor. This also may be used as a sleeping perch.

The Tutor

In most cases, young singers are taught by a good adult singing canary called a foresinger or a tutor, which is placed either in the aviary with the young cocks or in a cage placed close to the aviary wire.

When the old tutor sings, the young cocks will imitate him and try to be as good as, if not better than he is. However, it is better not to have a tutor at all than to have a bad one; otherwise, all of the young cocks will sing as badly.

The young cocks will not all have similar talents. Some will utter sounds that are too shrill and jarring; others will not be able to learn full tours. The experienced fancier will remove all of the inferior singers as soon as they are detected, until only the best ones remain. A tutor canary should be the same variety as its pupils, waterslager with waterslagers, Harz with Harz, and so on.

It is best to darken the "classroom" as much as possible so that the birds can concentrate on mimicking the songs. Just like human children, young canaries are easily distracted and would rather "play around" than concentrate on their "lessons." However, darkening is not always recommended as the still young birds must enjoy their freedom as much a possible, flying and frolicking as they wish. The tutor also should not use bad tones ("swearing"), as young canaries, just like children, soon will learn and repeat them.

If you do not have an excellent, first-class singing tutor, then you should try to reach your goal without

Battery of wooden song canary cages.

a tutor. This is really possible as the song is an inherited characteristic that need not necessarily be taught by a tutor. There are many fanciers whose birds have won singing prizes without having been taught by a tutor.

Young birds that first sing their full song with an almost closed beak and an inflated crop become the foresingers, and the other birds copy them. If they have faults, they are taken out of the hearing of the other birds. The inherited talent of these remaining birds thus can develop undisturbed and perhaps lead to unexpectedly good results.

This kind of training requires that the fancier be familiar with a good song. The recordings of good Harz, roller, and waterslagers can be purchased from specialist suppliers and these can be useful. Through listening carefully and frequently, the

fancier soon will learn to pick out a good singing bird.

Birds with a wide open beak, which repeatedly break their song and mostly start with high tours and notes, are practically worthless as songbirds. They should be separated from the other birds as soon as possible so that they do not affect the latter.

The Singing Cage

As soon as the young cocks have come fully through the first molt, they are each placed separately in a singing cage. The actual time of the year cannot be specific, because weather conditions, and thus the molt, vary from one location to another. If placed too early in the singing cage, the cock will go into a full molt, which should take place the following summer, and will not start singing. Before caging the young cocks, each one should be examined thoroughly. Each bird should be taken in the hand and the feathers blown aside, and if there are undeveloped feathers, it is still too early to cage a bird.

Every fancier who wishes to take part in bird shows will own one or more singing cases, with a number of compartments. At one time the fronts were enclosed by dark curtains, frequently green, to let the birds spend several hours each day in a darkened environment.

1. The cages should be cleaned thoroughly and the perches placed in easy reach of the food and water hoppers before the birds are introduced. The food and water hoppers also should be easy to service and not too high up in the cage.

2. The perch should be placed so that the bird's tail cannot touch the floor or walls. The young birds are not placed haphazardly in the singing case; on the contrary, family members, including the father (as foresinger), should be placed next to each other.

3. One should make sure that the birds are eating and drinking satisfactorily from the first day. After the first few days, in which the young birds will be getting accustomed to their new environment, the slides between the cages are not in position. As soon as they begin to try out their voices, the slides are placed into position to that each cage is out of view of the next.

4. The band number of each bird should be noted when it is placed in its singing cage and marked somewhere on the cage. This makes it more convenient to work out family relationships and so on.

5. The change from nursery to singing cage can be a traumatic one for the birds and can put them off for a while. They may lose their appetite somewhat, and a piece of stale bread in water may help to get them "back on their feet." Many breeders of song canaries feed their birds at this time with a little rape seed, a little canary grass seed, and a little rolled oats every day, supplemented two or three times a week with a dish of mixed weed seeds and some universal food. Do not forget a little fruit or green food.

6. As soon as the birds are feeding adequately and are used to their new cages, usually after about a week, close the curtains or doors of the singing cases for a few hours

Singing cages in a "suitcase"—ready for the show!

each day. Lengthen the period of darkness each day until the birds have light to feed only three times a day; of course, they also can find their food and drink in the darkened cage as it should not be pitch-black, just strongly shaded. The darkness is to keep the birds protected from distractions, so that they concentrate mainly on their singing practice. Birds with faulty songs soon can be picked out and removed, so that one can concentrate on the good singers.

7. When the singing reaches a certain stage, put four canary cages on a table in full light for about half an hour. Give each bird that sings a reward, such as a little niger seed. Calmly place birds that are in the light for ten minutes and do not sing, only eat, back in the singing case. Canaries have a certain amount of intelligence and soon learn that if they sing they get a reward and if they do not sing they are put back in the shady confines of the singing case. They learn the lesson quickly and the most intelligent birds will sing as soon as light is applied to them.

Note: The positions of the cages on the table, whether next to each other or on top of each other is immaterial, but they should have their positions changed and moved about as much as possible so that the birds quickly get used to new situations (for exhibitions). The singing case itself also should be moved about frequently so that the birds get accustomed to being transported.

By the end of November, the birds usually are ready for exhibition where singing contests are held. Each group of four birds should be placed frequently under artificial light so that they also get used to this medium. Each quartet gets a half hour to perform. If the birds are used to breaking into song each time they are placed in the light, wherever they may be, then the fancier will at least know that they will perform for the judges.

The Song of the Canary

The Harz or Roller Canary

The song of the wild canary has been developed in captivity over the last two centuries through purposeful intuition and strict selection of breeding pairs. The canary thus has evolved into a singing domesticated bird of which there is no parallel anywhere in the world.

At one time the fanciers recognized two types of song—the *Truttse* and the *Seifertse*—but these have been lost, so that today we speak of constant and nonconstant tours.

Rhythm and tone represent the song value of a canary, which it can emit in three ways: the roll, the bell, and the flute. The value of each tour is, within certain limits, determined by the depth of tone, the quality of sound, and fullness.

The whole canary song is called the *presentation* and consists of a chain of tours bound together with harmonious transitions. Each tour can be performed in different tone layers, and the deeper and fuller they are performed, the more valuable the bird.

The tours are categorized as follows:
- *Very good tours*, called hollow rolls, bass rolls, and water tours
- *Good tours*, called schockels, hollow bells, glucke tours, water rolls, and flutes
- *Fairly good tours*, called bells and bell rolls.

Hollow roll: The name originates from the hollow rolling character of this continuous tour, which can be regarded as the finest in the canary's repertoire. The hollow roll is sung with the vowels U (as in pure), O (as in bow), and OE as in (booth), and the consonant R, which should not be put in the foreground. The hollow roll can be further categorized into *straight*, *rising*, and *curved*. A good hollow roll is sung with a closed beak, as the opened beak releases a hard tone. A warbling tone is a fault.

Bass roll: This is the lowest tour in the repertoire and important; without this tour, the song is incomplete. The round, full, bass roll comes from a combination of the vowel O and the consonant R, where the beak is almost closed, and the sound comes from deep in the breast to be released forcefully. The R must not come to the fore, whereas the O must sound full and round. If other vowels are heard, this will minimize the quality of the tour. If the R comes to the fore, then the tone will be too hard. If a vowel A (as in bath) is heard, then the bass roll becomes

a flat bass roll. If the O and A are interchanged, a high bass roll is evident, and a loud bass roll—frequently with open beak often with an A (as in way) sound—is known as a click bass roll. All of these are classed as faults.

Schockel: In contrast to the above tours, the schockel is a broken tour, which is recognized by the jerky movements of the tones U, O, and OE, so that this tour can be compared with the neighing of a horse or the jerky laugh of a human. The tempo of the schockel should be slow and the space between tones is greater than in the hollow bell (see below). The schockel sounds can be prefixed with the H sound, for example, *hu-hoe*. If the consonants B or BL come into the song, then it may be called a water schockel. If a bird sings with an open beak, the value of the schockel is minimized.

Hollow bell: This tour is closely related to the schockel and possesses, in addition to the basic tones U, O, and OE, the consonants L and H. It frequently begins as a hollow roll with an R included, but is quickly replaced with an L. The sounds E (as in pet) and A (as in way) are classed as faults, and this tour also is sung with the beak barely opened; otherwise one would get a clappy hollow bell as the upper and lower mandibles beat together. Also at fault are the so-called slow and leaping hollow bell sounds, which arise from respectively greater and lesser interruption of the letter grouping. The more valuable are the U and OE tones, which suddenly sink from U to OE, and rise from OE to U.

Glucke: This tour is easy to recognize if it is performed well. The tour emerges from the breast through an almost closed beak. The ground tones are the U, the O, and the OE, with the consonants GLK, BLK, and KLK. There are various types, including the hollow gluck (with the OE), the water gluck (sounding like *klik*), the gluck bell (with a soft L), and the gluck roll (with an R between gluck tones).

Water roll: The value of the water roll lies in the fullness and depth of tones. It rarely is heard in the canary song, but must sound like water being tipped from a pure crystal decanter. The best ground tones are formed from U, O, and OE, and the consonants V, G, D, L, H, and B.

Flutes: Flutes are short tones, of medium volume and not too quick repetition. They are middle tours, but without flutes the canary's song is incomplete. There are three types of flutes: deep (with a DOE sound), medium (with a DU [as in bugle] sound), and high (with a DE [as in deep] sound). The deepest type is the best, but if the D is replaced by a T, this is regarded as a fault.

Bell tours: The bell tour sounds like a high-toned bell and is used as an alternation in the whole canary song. A good bell tour uses the vowel I (as in easily) and the consonant L, giving a metallic IL. The bell roll is a light hollow roll with an I and an R, frequently emitted by mediocre birds that can emit no proper hollow roll in their repertoire. All tours are considered faulty if emitted through an open beak, so even a beginner can spot this fault.

The Waterslager

The waterslagers, which are larger than the Harz and almost

Waterslager canaries.

And at the end the trophies...!!

always yellow in color, also possess a different style of song. In contrast to the soft rounded sounds of the Harz canary, the waterslager utters a beating sound with a metallic character, in which the rhythm is faster and the contrast between low and high notes is greater. The song is said to resemble that of a nightingale.

Some experts believe the Belgian waterslager was developed by German breeders, others think it was the Belgians who used a nightingale as a tutor. However, we do know that the Belgians have perfected the waterslager into the bird it is today.

The American Singer Canary

This "North American" was developed in the mid 1930s from a cross between a roller and a border fancy. The goal was to create a singer that had a louder voice that the roller.

Interest was so great that in 1943 the American Singer Club was inaugurated. The club indicates that its bird is a song-type canary bred in the United States by a systematic plan known as the blending of roller to border fancy over a period of years to produce a canary bird that has (1) an outstanding, free, harmonious song, pleasing to the ear, neither too loud nor too harsh, with plenty of variety; (2) a beautiful shape or type not over 5¾ inches (about 15 cm) long, with tight feathers, that will please the average home lover of canaries.

In order to reach this goal, the club issues its members with a carefully worked-out genetic chart; the goal is to have a strain of birds that is 69 percent roller and 31 percent border fancy.

The American singer is an attractive bird with a medium-sized beak, rounded head, pronounced shoulders, medium-length tail, wings, and legs—and all this on a small body. It should not have the roller's "dance" on the perch while singing, but should stand on the perch at an angle between 35 and 45 degrees, and, most important of all, should have a fearless disposition. This singer comes in many colors, but colors such as the red factor have implications for linebreeding operations. It usually takes some extra years to produce a solid strain. The American singer delivers its song while perched; a roller will sing while moving. The breed is not as popular as the roller but the ranks of its followers grows rapidly each year. They are judged against their own national standards.

Useful Literature and Addresses

Books

Dodwell, G. T. *The Complete Book of Canaries*. New York: Howell Book House, Inc., 1986.

Frisch, Otto von. *Canaries*. Hauppauge, New York: Barron's Educational Series, Inc., 1999.

La Rosa, Don. *How to Build Everything You Need for Your Birds*. Smithtown, New York: Audubon Publishing Company, 1983.

Rittrich-Dorenkamp, Sigrun. *Canaries, Family Pet Series*. Hauppauge, New York: Barron's Educational Series, Inc., 1999.

Vriends, Matthew M. *Simon & Schuster's Guide to Pet Birds*, 10th ed. New York: Simon & Schuster, 1998.

——. *The New Bird Handbook*. Hauppauge, New York: Barron's Educational Series, Inc., 1989.

——. *Hand-feeding and Raising Baby Birds*. Hauppauge, New York: Barron's Educational Series, Inc., 1996.

—— and Tanya M. Heming-Vriends *Hancock House Encyclopedia of Estrildid Finches*. Blaine, WA 2002.

Walker, G. B. R. and Dennis Avon. *Coloured, Type and Song Canaries*. London: Blanford Press, Artillery House, 1986.

Magazines

Bird Talk
P.O. Box 6050
Mission Veijo, California 92690

Journal of the Association of Avian Veterinarians
P.O. Box 811720
Boca Raton, Florida 33481-1720

The AFA Watchbird
P.O. Box 56218
Phoenix, Arizona 85079-6218

Index